"Esposito provides an evidenced-based framework for small- and medium-sized businesses to strengthen execution and optimize long-term success. These businesses are the backbone of the economy and must navigate a unique set of questions and challenges that are often overlooked or underestimated yet carry significant consequences if not addressed. The wisdom and experience captured in this book provides a tailored blueprint for leaders in this strategically important business sector as they chart the course for a stronger future."

—**Brad D. Smith,** president, Marshall University,
and former chairman and CEO, Intuit

"Every chief executive officer or president who recognizes that growth for their businesses and their careers will come through expanding knowledge and deepening understanding of what drives success and failure for businesses should read *The Structure of Success*. Patrick Esposito's research, insights, and frameworks combine to create a compelling and lasting resource for executive leaders that can help guide crucial decisions and actions to help position their enterprises for long-term, sustained success."

—**Xavier Mufraggi,** former CEO, YPO

The
Structure
of
Success

A Framework to Help
Build Your Business Better

PATRICK ESPOSITO

AN INC.
ORIGINAL

An Inc. Original
New York, New York
www.anincoriginal.com

This work is being published under the An Inc. Original imprint by an exclusive arrangement with Inc. Magazine. Inc. Magazine and the Inc. logo are registered trademarks of Mansueto Ventures, LLC. The An Inc. Original logo is a wholly owned trademark of Mansueto Ventures, LLC.

Distributed by Greenleaf Book Group

For ordering information or special discounts for bulk purchases, please contact Greenleaf Book Group at PO Box 91869, Austin, TX 78709, 512.891.6100.

Design and composition by Greenleaf Book Group
Cover design by Greenleaf Book Group

Publisher's Cataloging-in-Publication data is available.

Print ISBN: 978-1-63909-018-1

eBook ISBN: 978-1-63909-019-8

To offset the number of trees consumed in the printing of our books, Greenleaf donates a portion of the proceeds from each printing to the Arbor Day Foundation. Greenleaf Book Group has replaced over 50,000 trees since 2007.

Printed in the United States of America on acid-free paper

23 24 25 26 27 28 29 30   10 9 8 7 6 5 4 3 2 1

First Edition

*This book is dedicated to my wife, Michelle Varga Esposito,
and my daughters, Natalie Esposito and Elizabeth Esposito, each
of whom inspires me daily. It is also dedicated to my parents,
Dr. Patrick Esposito and Caroline Esposito, for their
early encouragement to work hard.*

CONTENTS

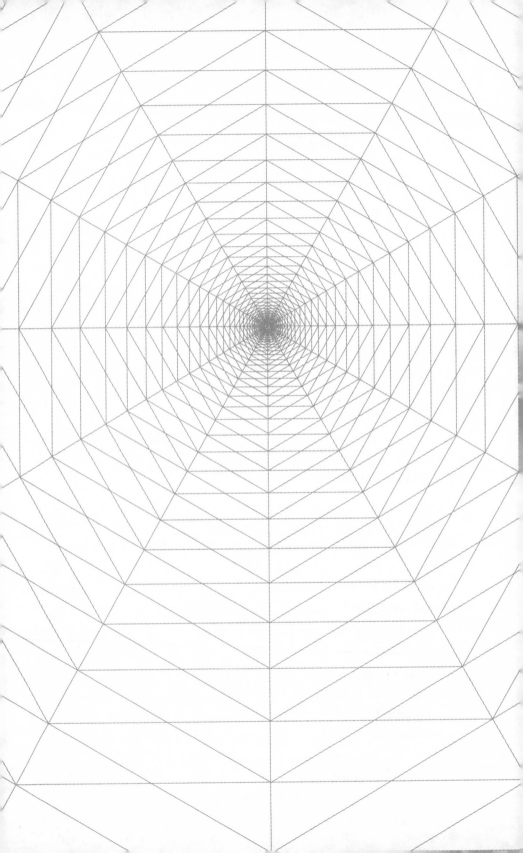

INTRODUCTION

Success versus failure. As the leader of a start-up, small business, family business, or a team within a larger organization, you face a constant battle. It is the clash between what you seek versus what you fear. It is the struggle that you face day in and day out. It is the conflict that occupies your conscious thoughts as you work and, likely, even when you find time to distance yourself from work. It is—for many of us—what keeps us up at night.

How exactly, though, can you achieve your business goals and aspirations without stumbling along the way or falling victim to a complete collapse?

The answer is really quite simple: You need to have a relentless focus on building and rebuilding your business better and stronger by focusing on making critical and strategic decisions to create the conditions for success from inside your business.

Building and rebuilding your business should be second nature to you. You are a builder at your core. You are a creator of jobs, teams, products, services, communities, and wealth. Each of us wants to make our business—or businesses, for the serial entrepreneurs among us—stronger with each passing day, every passing year, and every reinvention.

The best part about leading a business is that you are never really done with the work of improving your ventures. You always have a chance to make your venture stronger. By focusing on the internal and foundational issues of your business, you create opportunities for success and minimize the risks of failure.

But how should you design and advance the circumstances in which your business or businesses can flourish? That is always the question a business faces at each phase of its existence.

The reason you want to succeed is usually easy to pinpoint. Maybe you want to make your business function more efficiently, grow more jobs, produce more profits, be more resilient, or secure your family's future. Maybe you just want to be able to sleep through each night and be less worried about the future.

Creating successes—whether you define success as sustainment, growth, an exit, or something else—usually comes down to taking a disciplined approach to building and rebuilding your business using a simple framework for assessing, deciding on, planning for, and implementing initiatives focused on its key structural components. Using the framework to undertake this analysis and make decisions will help you and your business—or businesses—design and implement the plans needed to survive and thrive.

The internal structures you select and use to operate your business will, ultimately, do more to drive positive outcomes and help you manage risks and threats than most of the other decisions you make or actions you take. By focusing on making critical decisions about these internal components and implementing the decisions in an efficient and effective way, you will make sure that you generate success and avoid failure, regardless of the risks and threats you face or the opportunities and prospects you seize.

Ready for the Expected and the Unexpected

The COVID-19 pandemic probably taught you that you cannot predict everything you and your business will face. This pandemic probably also taught you that you can be ready to assess, determine, plan, and implement strategies for change and that you can have strategies and tactics prepared and ready for change when something unforeseen hits. You may have learned that having a strong framework and structural components can help support your preparations and responses. The pandemic may have taught you that negative business impacts often come not from the unexpected changes you face but from a lack of internal readiness to respond to those changes.

Sometimes it is not a major event—like a pandemic or a global recession—that impacts or threatens your business. Events can be localized but still unpredictable, like natural disasters or human-made threats to the safety and security of your business. Threats can also be specific to your business sector—like new market participants with innovative models that upend business as usual or new regulations that alter your future opportunities.

More often, though, these shifts can come from inside your business—like personnel changes, dynamics that require the splintering of a once-great business partnership, or growth without the necessary internal capacity. Or these changes can be circumstances that touch you personally—like an unforeseen health issue, burnout, or the simple realization that you are spread too thin to drive the outcomes you and your business need.

As you know, change is not necessarily negative. It could be an opportunity to achieve greatness—by pivoting your business or your business products to generate growth or to save your business. Or it may require you to plan for expansion by adding new offerings and creating new internal infrastructure to support the further development of your business to capitalize on potential growth.

Your next phase could be the opportunity to sell your business, merge your business, or acquire a new business to become part of something even greater than the one you are leading now. The odds are pretty good that you have seen change approaching in different forms during your business career.

In any of these scenarios, if you have a strong underlying framework and structural components, you will be prepared and ready to respond in a way that helps your business continue to succeed.

Although this book is not a crystal ball that will alert you when change is afoot, it will help you develop your ability to lead and manage your business at all stages by showing you how to develop strong structural components through a simple framework of proven approaches, methodologies, and tools. This book will serve as a guide to help drive your success, and it will offer suggestions in hopes of steering you away from failure. And if you are a serial entrepreneur or family business leader like me, this book will help you throughout your business career.

Why This Book?

During my twenty years founding and operating small businesses and advising leaders of other small- and medium-sized businesses, the main difference between achieving success and falling prey to failure has—time and time again—revolved around being ready for whatever is next, which might be anything from an evolution of the business to a revolution in the global economy. I have learned that businesses are successful when their leaders use a simple framework for architecting internal structural components to build stronger, more resilient businesses and to create the conditions for successful outcomes.

All of us—the entrepreneurs, the family business leaders, the start-up executives, and those who aspire to build and manage businesses—know all too well the results of not being ready for change. And if you are a leader of a small- or medium-sized business, whether you are aiming for high growth and an exit or a sustainable family venture, you likely have experienced the feelings of being overwhelmed, suffering from a chronic shortage of time, and falling into reactive rather than proactive modes of operation.

We have all probably experienced some of the symptoms: stress-induced insomnia, sleepless nights grinding away on the next necessary activity, high blood pressure or other health issues, missed time with family, losing touch with friends, and feeling alone on an island of self-doubt and worry. Have you reflected on what causes these concerns for you?

Usually, it comes down to the epic battle of success versus failure.

Based on research and analysis detailed in this book, eight critical questions will help you focus on the inner workings of your business. Answering these questions will help you create the structure to position your business for success.

1. How should I build my governance structure and team to meet my business goals without risking my culture, current freedoms, and successful trajectory?

2. How can I build the right management team, and what is the best way to engage and compensate my team members to meet my business goals?

3. How should I adjust or pivot my business strategy to achieve my goals?

4. What is the best way to build infrastructure to support growth without killing profitability or sacrificing the engines that are driving my business?

5. How should I manage business disputes or breakups with my business partners when relationships become frayed?

6. Should I examine opportunities to advance to an acquisition of a partner or competitor, merge with a partner or competitor, sell my business, divest a part of my business, or make a new investment to help my business (and when should I do it)?

7. What disasters may arise in the future, how should I prepare for these obstacles, and if I am experiencing a crisis now, how should I manage it?

8. What happens to my business and my family's livelihood when it is time for me (or key management team members) to retire or, worse, meet an untimely demise?

These eight questions about critical and strategic business decisions are focused on what happens inside the business. They are also the ones that have usually—in some form or another—kept me up at night. These same questions have also confounded my friends, my colleagues, and the business owners I have worked with and advised over the course of my career.

Your answers to these eight questions will guide your decisions about the core internal components of your business. Those decisions will help you achieve your business goals and position yourself for success—with fewer sleepless nights. You will also create a business that is strong and resilient in the face of risks and threats and poised to seize opportunities as they arise.

Your answers to the questions related to the internal structural components that form the core of your business are not immovable, permanent, or unchangeable. Additional key questions and structural components may be critical to your business or businesses, based on your unique circumstances. The structural components you will create using the framework presented in this book are malleable. They are meant to be reexamined, and they may need to be extended as your business grows or encounters headwinds.

Why is it that most of us struggle with the same concerns and yet find it challenging to address them, despite these common threads? A good friend who is a second-generation family business leader likes to remind me that "most business books are not really business books for most of us." He is absolutely correct—especially for those of us who help lead the more than 99 percent of businesses that are small businesses, which range from multigenerational family businesses to venture-backed start-ups and from professional service firms to solo freelancers.

Put simply, there is a business book alignment problem for us. Many of the business books lauded by the experts and consumed voraciously by us do not really apply to the types of businesses that many of us operate.

As we know all too well, business books tend to concentrate on outliers like Silicon Valley and its high-risk/high-reward scenarios, massive publicly traded companies, and other exceptional stories. Those books help us learn how to build "gazelles and unicorns," "go public," and manage billion-dollar companies. Unfortunately, those ventures are usually extreme case studies and are far removed from the businesses in which most of us make our livelihoods, provide for our families, and build our communities.

Worse still, most business books that focus on the outliers tend to treat the symptoms, not the disease. Instead of providing a framework that helps us foster success by systemically rebuilding our business, the authors of these "symptom management programs" sell us a panacea for our business issues. They sell us quick fixes that overemphasize the "treatment" of one pain point in our business—sales, marketing, people processes, et cetera. These quick fixes do not put us on a path to long-term improvement. Rather (and unfortunately so), many of the books that focus on our businesses offer us ways to manage our pain through treatment programs that can help improve small pieces of our businesses, but they never really help us overcome the core structural problems that plague our ventures.

This book, however, will provide you with a lasting resource that can help guide your assessments, decisions, planning, and implementations for the critical and strategic activities that you and your business ventures will face. This book will help you position your business ventures for long-term, sustained success.

During my career, I have had the privilege of supporting nearly one hundred companies and other organizations in various ways, from assessing how to build and rebuild their businesses to supporting the building of new business-oriented organizations within the U.S. Department of Defense. The tenets in this book are fit for battle and ready for you to use to benefit you and your business ventures as you prepare for whatever lies ahead.

This book will not provide perfect solutions to all your business issues. But I hope that reading it and applying the approaches, methodologies, and tools it contains will allow you to sleep better at night, improve your time management, and strengthen your business outcomes. In short, I hope this framework and the structural components you design with it help you as you continue to lead your business ventures.

This book focuses on small- and medium-sized businesses, but the core principles have been applied in advisory work to support large companies, publicly traded companies, venture-backed start-ups, nonprofits, and government agencies. So, even if you are not part of a small- or medium-sized business and are wondering whether this book is for you, I encourage you to continue reading. Most larger organizations are beginning to adopt operating models that draw from small businesses. Further, based on my experiences with larger clients, the leaders of these organizations have benefited from applying these concepts in their activities.

What Is Ahead and Why It Matters

Some of you may be thinking, *I like the idea of sleeping better, having more time for the things that matter, driving stronger business performance, and achieving success rather than failure. But how will this book help me?*

In the chapters ahead, I first set out the key tenets of the framework. Then I apply these elements to eight critical and strategic decision categories. In these chapters I do the following:

- Examine how the broad universe of your fellow small- and medium-sized business leaders approach (or ignore to their detriment) these critical and strategic decision categories

- Show how successful business leaders approach these decision categories

- Share some relevant anecdotal stories

- Prompt some self-examination of yourself and your business to help you create the structural components that will position your business for success

Chapter 1 starts with a brief examination of your business journey and asks you to reflect on the experiences, successes, and failures you have faced thus far. This is an exploration of your specific business context. The chapter then shifts to prepare you for the work ahead by laying out the context for thinking and acting in a way that supports the approaches, methodologies, and tools that will help you position your business ventures for success. The chapter also provides some comparative analysis of how expert business leaders prepare to establish conditions for success.

Chapter 2 provides you with the core approaches, methodologies, and tools that can be applied throughout all stages of your business ventures and business career—starting up, scaling up, breaking up, handing off, and others. These tools will help you chart a course for success and navigate around failure. This chapter is designed to help you identify, prepare for, and manage any and all of the issues and opportunities you face in the months, years, and decades ahead. It gives you a practical and efficient approach that ensures that thoughtfulness does not generate paralysis through analysis.

While Chapter 1 and Chapter 2 focus on the context, models, and conditions for positioning your business ventures for success, Chapter 3 examines the causes of failures and offers insights from a survey of market leaders and expert business leaders. The chapter looks at how the present-day drivers of failures align with failures over time. This prepares you for the work ahead and supports you in your battle for success over failure.

Next, we will begin to apply the framework's approaches, methodologies, and tools to eight critical and strategic decision categories related to the internal structures of the business:

1. Governance models and governance team composition

2. Management team models, composition, engagement, and compensation

3. Adjustments and pivots

4. Growth and infrastructure development

5. Business disputes and breakups

6. Acquisitions, mergers, exits, and other business transactions

7. Disaster preparedness and management

8. Succession planning

In Chapter 4, we apply the core framework to explore why governance and your governance team composition are vital to your business. We examine options for governance that will support you and your business as it grows. We also look at ways to consider the composition of your governance team and think about how it complements your own capabilities and biases.

In Chapter 5, we turn from governance to your management models, composition, and compensation. We apply the core approaches, methodologies, and tools to a specific decisional domain. In this instance, we examine how to consider management team growth, composition, engagement, and compensation in a way that actually aligns with business goals, rather than simply top-line and bottom-line financial figures.

Next, we look at how to apply the framework to your core business activities. In Chapter 6, we explore business adjustment and pivot options and make decisions about how best to position your business for the future. We also examine how to best consider opportunities and constraints.

In Chapter 7, we look at how to apply the core concepts to develop your business infrastructure in a way that supports growth without strangling the opportunity for more growth. In doing so, we will look at what infrastructure limitations might be viable and what non-investments will kill your business and burn out your team.

Next, we will explore ownership changes in two chapters. The first of these two chapters—Chapter 8—focuses on business disputes and break-ups between partners. We examine how to prepare for these scenarios before they happen and provide options for working through the difficulties and breakups without negatively affecting your business or your career.

The second of these two chapters—Chapter 9—focuses on ownership changes and examines acquisitions, mergers, exits, and other business transactions. Here, we discuss how to explore the multiple pathways for growth through a systematic and regularized process without distracting you and your team from the core business operations.

The final chapters focus on decision categories to explore the certainties that every sustained business will face—disasters and succession. In Chapter 10, which focuses on disaster preparedness and management, we explore how to assess and plan for threats, respond to these challenges, and revisit these plans pragmatically.

In Chapter 11, which targets succession planning, we focus on addressing one of the most challenging areas for a business leader to rationally approach—how to position the business for when you or key members of your management team are no longer there. We explore emergency and long-term succession plans, options for designing these plans, and ways to ensure the plans can be studied and reassessed before circumstances dictate the need for implementation.

By the time you finish this book, you will know how to prioritize getting ready for everything that you, your team, and your business will face. My hope is that you will be able to apply what you have learned in each chapter and feel better prepared to navigate each stage of your business so you can position—using a strong structure—your business ventures (and you) for success rather than failure.

PATRICK ESPOSITO
Morgantown, West Virginia

1

THE CONTEXT

"The road to success and the road to
failure are almost exactly the same."

—SIR COLIN R. DAVIS

Reflecting on your journey in business—whether dedicated to a single
venture or a series of businesses—probably easily evokes vividly detailed
memories about the times when you built things well, the times when
you needed to rebuild your business completely, and the times in between
when some minor or moderate changes were needed to ensure that your
business survived or was back on a path to success.

Undoubtedly, the experiences you had in your life prior to your current business pathway—where you grew up, how you were raised, what
outside exposures you had, what jobs you performed, and your business
experiences, among other factors—provide both perspective and bias that
influence your decisions about business structures and how to prepare for
building and rebuilding your business ventures.

Whether you have just started your first business or have been grinding away for two decades, being able to examine your experiences, the lessons you learned, and how your experiences formed your current views is incredibly important as you prepare for what lies ahead when you work to build your business better.

This book can be an asset to those deciding whether to start a new business venture, but it is not intended to help with the hard work related to the critical and strategic decisions needed for the initiation of new ventures. The business launch phase is so complex and important that it merits a separate, dedicated book.

In this book, we center our attention on the business activities that occur after you have already launched a business venture. The reason is simple: The stakes are high when you are deciding to launch a business, but the stakes are even higher when you are already leading a business. With that leadership role comes responsibilities for meeting your family's financial needs, providing financial opportunities for your business partners and team members, offering opportunities for professional growth and development for your team members, and other responsibilities.

In short, once the business has launched, your journey is not just about pursuing your dreams and realizing those dreams for yourself, your family, and your team members. It is about fighting against the specters and demons that keep you up at night. It is about building and rebuilding your business—from the inside—each day.

I launched my first business venture more than twenty years ago with my then significant other (now my spouse) and my father. Later, we added one of my best friends and a team of high-achieving and hardworking souls to the mix. When we launched, I was rather naive and did not understand just how much the odds were stacked against success. Nor did I understand how much thought, how many adjustments, and how much effort building, growing, and trying to survive would take. I am sure that many of you can empathize.

Before we start exploring the framework and structures that support sustained success, we are going to look deeply at the context of your past business experiences and the context for your future use of the approaches, methodologies, and tools that will help to position you and your business ventures to win again and again.

The Personal Context

When you contemplate your future in business, it is important to consider your current mindset, the past journey that led you to where you are today, and where you want to be in the future. In your mind, retrace your path. Consider the great times, your biggest wins, the tough times, the failures, why you are a business leader, and how you define success and failure. For example:

- Why did you choose this path in life? Why do you stay on this course?

- What brings you the most joy? What causes the greatest frustration?

- What do you too easily fall prey to, time and again? What do you want the outcome of your life's work in business to be?

- What do you consider success to be? What do you deem to be a failure?

While you ponder the answers to these questions, I will provide some of my personal context. This will give you a window into my background as we work through this book together.

I did not set out to spend my life in business. In fact, I had a very different vision for my personal trajectory. From very early on in my formative years, I wanted to serve others through public service. After very brief stints as an attorney in private practice and in state government, I realized that it was difficult to escape my entrepreneurial genes. I saw that the call to service was leading me away from a life as a public servant and into a role in which I attempted to create jobs in a region of the country that sorely lacked new businesses. I did not really choose this path as much as it chose me.

Ask yourself why you started your business career and your path. Maybe you were taking over the reins of a family business. Perhaps starting your own business had always been your dream. Or, like me, perhaps your path chose you. Whatever the reason, I am sure there was a learning curve.

For me, once I was on my path, I endured a baptism by fire that shaped me, guided my direction, and forged the path I have followed for the past two decades. This journey has been full of thinking, tinkering, massive missteps, big gambles, and lessons learned. Given the risks and rewards, why do I stay? Maybe it is inertia. Or perhaps, like any risk-taker, I find it hard to walk away from the potential to achieve successes that are even bigger than the one I have just achieved. Truthfully, it is probably a little of both of those factors combined with the belief that with all I have learned from my experiences, I can build the next business better than the last one.

Maybe you have a similar belief that what you started can be more than it is today. Or perhaps working in this business venture is the only job you have ever known, which is why you stay on your journey. I realize that I genuinely love winning and building successful business ventures—personally, for my teammates, and for my family. It is achievement that brings me joy. Maybe this is because I participated in too many academic competitions as a child or too many team sports throughout my life. But I realize that I am, to some extent, hopelessly addicted to the pursuit of success. It is what defines my self-worth, perhaps to an almost detrimental point. But it is also what drives me to work hard every day. Maybe you are wired similarly?

When I look at what causes me pain, it is the flip side of what compels me to work: failure. One hundred percent of the time, failure. But maybe not the type of failure you expect. I do not care about making mistakes. Errors and missteps will happen. What brings me pain is negatively impacting the lives of team members—having to terminate people's employment or losing investment funds for financial backers.

I recognize that failure is what brings me dread. Unfortunately, I also tend to create opportunities for it to arise. After twenty years of business leadership, I realize that I often create my own trouble. Idea generation has never been difficult for me, but avoiding distraction and moving from creation to execution is a constant struggle. In fact, during the writing (and rewriting) of this book, I worked with business partners to pivot a business and launch two more businesses. As you may have guessed, I fall prey to being a little undisciplined in the search for business success. (And, yes, I am working on using this book to help keep me, my business partners, and my businesses more disciplined.) Maybe you, too, have similar traps you see reappearing.

Perhaps the most important topic to consider as you and I examine our business journeys together is what we want to achieve for the future. I want to help you create successes and avoid failures. Those themes—success and failure—are still what keep me up at night.

We each define what success and failure look like for ourselves and for our business ventures. Sometimes the definition of success or failure changes. As you consider your business and how to rebuild it better or how to improve your multiple business ventures, the alignment of your plans for the foundations of your business with your vision of success and failure will be critically important. Because of their importance, we will consider your definitions of these terms frequently throughout this book.

With the benefit of having counseled a range of businesses on various types of decisions, two things have become clear: (1) success—whatever it means to you—is primarily created and (2) failure—however you view it—is avoided by creating the right conditions for building a stronger business, thus establishing the structure of success.

The Additional Context

In my experience, optimal conditions are created by using a strong framework and focusing on eight critical and strategic decision categories that likely will best position you and your business for success. To make the best choices in these decision categories, it may be important to expand your context for decision-making and develop a mindset that focuses on leveraging insights from others and embracing constructive and efficient actions. We cannot completely distance ourselves from our past, but we can attempt to integrate that past context into a new future context.

Your future context starts with developing or reembracing faith in yourself and directing your energy to constructive and efficient actions, with an emphasis on the following actions:

- Building from the ground up

- Worrying productively

- Embracing change

- Trusting yourself and your team

- Making the commitment

In preparing for this future context, we will explore some research related to some of the areas of emphasis. We will also examine some research conducted in support of this book, which was undertaken to ensure that the concepts I believe to be important are considered important by our successful business leader peers. To test the concepts detailed in this book, we conducted a survey of leaders from one hundred businesses who are recognized as experts for their accomplishments. To provide some context for the results of the survey, some background on the participants may be helpful.

The leaders played critical roles in founding, scaling, and operating these businesses. Nearly 60 percent of these leaders were serving as executive leaders of the businesses at the time. A majority of these leaders were also founders of the businesses they lead, while roughly 40 percent were business owners who no longer served as executive leaders. These leaders were drawn from diverse industries, including technology; professional services; retail and hospitality; industrial, manufacturing, and construction; media; financial services; energy, utilities, and natural resources;

transportation and logistics; and other market segments. Of these leaders, 70 percent have co-founders and/or co-owners in their businesses, while 30 percent did not. In addition, of the leaders with co-founders and co-owners we surveyed, 9 percent were engaged in family businesses.

The sizes of the businesses ranged from start-ups and small businesses with one to twenty employees to small- to medium-sized businesses with up to 250 employees. The surveyed businesses were roughly equally distributed among three size classes: one to twenty employees; twenty-one to fifty employees, and fifty-one to 250 employees. The ages of these businesses varied and had an average of 11.3 years from their founding. Not quite half of the businesses had been in operation for more than ten years (and therefore had demonstrated a strong ability to sustain success). Of these businesses, 19 percent had been in operation for twenty years or more, 10 percent had been in active existence for sixteen to twenty years, and 17 percent had been operating for eleven to fifteen years. Just over half of the businesses had been operating for less than ten years—38 percent had been in operation for five to ten years, and 16 percent had existed for less than five years. This distribution of business size and age provides a reasonable distribution of survey points to ensure that we do not have a strong bias in the opinions toward any particular business size or age.

Throughout this book, we will look at the results of our survey of these leaders to gain insights into how they approach the shared road that can lead to both success and failure. For now, we will examine the main additional elements—beyond our personal experiences—that should underscore our decision-making context.

Building from the Ground Up

Building is something we have been doing since we were very young. Most likely our parents provided us with wooden blocks or pop beads initially, and tangrams or LEGO bricks later.

You probably witnessed your parents, grandparents, or older siblings developing plans and implementing those plans. You might have even helped them. Perhaps it was the design and development of a physical structure. Maybe it was something closer to home, like the plan for a family reunion.

These early toys and formative observational experiences not only provided us with great memories but also instilled in us the framework for the critical executive thinking required to be a great business leader. These activities made us the builders we are today. But how?

Research by Dr. Amy Shelton, a cognitive psychologist, at the Johns Hopkins University Science of Learning Institute, provides some insights about the value of these early toys. If you are a parent, her insights may make the stabbing pain in your foot when you accidentally step on a stray LEGO brick seem worthwhile. As reported by Maria Blackburn, Dr. Shelton and her team at Johns Hopkins University studied children at the university's Center for Talented Youth. "When kids are building with blocks and Legos, they're using spatial reasoning skills . . . [that] not only have a relationship to academics, but to the fields you might gravitate to, and where you're going to excel," opined Shelton. Even more intriguing was the conclusion that Blackburn attributed to Shelton and her research group based on a study in which children were shown an example of a LEGO structure, given LEGO bricks, and asked to build a similar structure. Dr. Shelton's team used electronic devices to track the LEGO bricks and collect data on how the children build structures. Her team discovered that experience matters in terms of building strong structures. "Master builders [kids with a lot of LEGO-building experience] were deliberate in their movements and generally built structures from the bottom up."[1]

Fascinating, right? Even among children, the "master builders" create "structures from the bottom up."

While Shelton and her team are focused on the implications of these spatial skills for the next generation of scientists, technologists, engineers,

---

1   Maria Blackburn, "How Legos and Blocks Help Make Your Child Smarter," Johns Hopkins University Hub, March 7, 2016, https://hub.jhu.edu/2016/03/07/lego-blocks-build-better-thinkers/.

and mathematicians, there are obvious implications for business leaders in any field. As we all know, every structure needs to be built with a solid foundation, and anytime you rebuild that structure, you really should check to make sure that the foundation is still strong.

Worrying Productively

You should check the foundation of your business ventures, but you should avoid checking too much. You should worry—at least a little. Not in a way that lets the worry consume you, but in a way that leads to better plans and better outcomes.

In my experience, constructive worry is often the difference between success and failure. "Constructive" is the key, though. What is "constructive worry"? It is worrying that focuses on looking at issues that may impact you and your business and coupling this examination of issues with potential mitigation measures. It takes a negative possibility and couples it with potential ways to alleviate the obstacle.

I come from a long line of worriers. My paternal Italian grandmother worried about everything—death or injury from car or air travel, car accidents in the initial minutes of a rainstorm due to the oils emerging from the asphalt roads, brain injuries from minor bumps on the head, falling down steps by running too fast, judgment from others about what she had said in a recent phone call, and my grandfather's business ventures. You name it, she worried about it. The same tendencies existed in her son, my father. I have that same potential to over-worry, unless I am careful to manage it and try to make my worrying habits constructive.

Maybe you come from a long line of worriers, too. Or maybe you are one now that you are running your own business.

Worry can be fantastic and help you see the world more clearly if harnessed properly. Alternatively, it can lead to mental health issues, physical health issues, relationship issues, and business issues.

I am not alone in believing that the right amount of worry and the right approach to worrying can yield great results. Many academic researchers have focused on studying the pitfalls and potential of worrying. Among them are Dr. Kate Sweeny, a psychology researcher at the University of California–Riverside, who has been cited by media outlets such as the BBC and NBC.

In a paper by Sweeny and her then doctoral advisee, Michael D. Dooley, they posit that "despite its faults, worry has an upside. It serves a motivating function by drawing attention to situations that require action, keeping the need for action salient, and promoting critical examination of one's options for goal-directed action. . . . Worrying the right amount is better than not worrying at all."[2]

If you are a worrier, this book will help you channel that worry into positive action. If you are not a worrier, it will empower you to begin worrying productively.

Embracing Change

If you have mastered the concepts of building from the ground up and worrying productively, the next concept to consider is the need to embrace change and to do so proactively.

Face it—change is really hard. No matter how many times you have been forced to make changes, it is difficult. It requires energy, focus, and being comfortable with something new.

In my own business career, I had to embrace change when I realized that the business plan that had carried our first start-up through its first few years of operation was not working anymore due to external factors. And I realized that it was never going to work—at least not at that time. That cold reality drove the need to embrace change and to diligently commit to doing it right. More details on that saga will follow in the chapter on adjustments and pivots, but the cold truth of

---

2   Kate Sweeny and Michael D. Dooley, "The Surprising Upsides of Worrying," *Social and Personality Psychology Compass*, April 18, 2017, https://doi.org/10.1111/spc3.12311.

reaching the point where you must make a decision about whether you want to sustain your business—which includes the jobs and incomes of your team, the funds that your investors dedicated to your business, and your own livelihood—or call it a day will certainly ensure that you decide to embrace change.

Whether it was actually first said by the ancient Greek philosopher Heraclitus or some other insightful thinker during his time or before, you have heard it in countless forms: "Change is the only constant." But while you have taken this truth of transitions as fact, have you truly welcomed change and made it part of your business processes? More to the point, do you have processes in place for assessing, determining, planning, and implementing change in your business?

To be clear, when we speak of the processes that allow you and your business to truly embrace change, we are not looking at whether you have strategic planning or change management initiatives in place. Those programs tend to focus on managing, planning, and implementing, instead of on the critical step of assessing. Rather, we are seeking to understand whether you truly have mechanisms for identifying the inputs needed to analyze the changes that will impact your business in a way that actually informs the decision-making, planning, and implementation.

We all likely have been part of organizational strategic planning activities that do not provide a reasonable mechanism for assessing both external factors that will precipitate changes and organizational factors—both external and internal—that will drive the need for change. Unfortunately, decision-making, planning, and implementation without proper processes for assessment lead to flawed structures for our businesses and to business structures built on weak foundations.

While this concept of a strong assessment prior to planning seems intuitive, does our sample group of expert business leaders support this approach? Nearly 70 percent of our surveyed group of business leaders responded that they have processes in place for all four facets of this approach for embracing change, as shown in Figure 1.1.

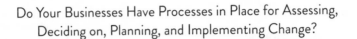

Do Your Businesses Have Processes in Place for Assessing, Deciding on, Planning, and Implementing Change?

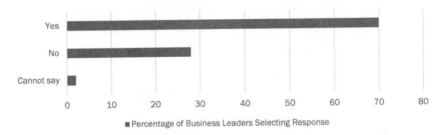

Figure 1.1

Trusting Yourself and Your Team

How should you go about your assessment, decision-making, planning, and implementation activities? Do you outsource these activities to an outside consultant or team of consultants? The answer is no—at least, do not ask them to actually do the activities for you.

If you believe that you need to hire a consultant or team of consultants to do the work of assessing, deciding, planning, and implementing changes for your business on an outsourced basis, you should probably fire yourself and your team. I am joking (a little), because there *is* value in having consultants assist you with some of the work that you and your team need to do—such as helping to inform your work with research and insights or providing a framework for the work that you and your team will do. But you and your team need to do the actual work of assessing, deciding, planning, and implementing.

After all, who knows your business and the environment around it better than you and your team? No one. You need to trust your team—your business partners, your management team, your security council, and your professional advisors—to diligently grind through the analytical tasks that will drive your business forward.

Should you consider hiring consultants or other experts to help you understand potential problems and opportunities that should be factored into your assessment, decision-making, planning, and implementation activities? What about engaging consultants to provide you and your team with a framework for assessing, decision-making, planning, and implementation? Well, maybe that is a "yes."

Why "maybe"? The answer depends on two key items: (1) how confident you are in your ability to gather the information and establish the frameworks needed to make the assessments and (2) whether you have the time to gather the information and establish the frameworks needed for the activities. If you feel like you cannot gather the inputs and frameworks needed for assessment and decision-making, then you should definitely consider relying on outside consultants to support your assessment, decision-making, planning, and implementation. Engaging consultants for these tasks should only supplement the work of your team, not displace it.

Why is this practice of trusting your team so critical?

A business associate once likened the results of an assessment, decision-making, planning, and implementation process entrusted to consultants to the creation of a "Frankenstein from a mad scientist laboratory." His view—which is 100 percent right—is that any process that determines where the business is going that does not rely on the team that will be expected to operationalize the results of the decision-making and planning will fail to be executed in an effective and efficient way. Worse, an over-involvement of consultants in these processes often leads to unrealistic assessments, decision-making, planning, and implementation that are built on flawed data and information about the business and its operational context—detailed information that only your team members possess.

You and your team should regularly do the work to assess, decide, plan, and implement your new business initiatives. It is vitally important to your business success. Do you want some additional validation? Look no further than our business leader survey group for additional confirmation.

How do our expert business leaders approach their reassessments of their business model, plans, and strategies? Do they focus on regularly working with their team? Yes, they do, and very much so, including normalized reviews with their management team, board of directors, business partners, and advisors. A small group—less than 10 percent—do not focus on regularly revisiting these core business structures. The full results from this question are provided in Figure 1.2.

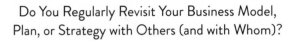

Figure 1.2

Making the Commitment

How often should you examine or reexamine your business model, plan, or strategy with these assessment, decision-making, planning, and implementation structures?

In my work advising small businesses and their leadership teams, I tend to recommend the same approach that has worked for me and the businesses that I help lead—a regularly scheduled review with the flexibility to revisit the plans when events or issues arise. For most companies, this means an annual plan with quarterly reviews and additional reviews based on issues that arise and opportunities that are presented.

To be clear, an annual plan is not and should not be a fixed, immovable object. An important concept to master is that you need to own the plan, not let the plan own you. Plans are good, but the entire point of revisiting the models, plans, and strategies is to make changes—not just to your business, but also to your models, plans, and strategies.

What should you do to commit to creating a strong process for continually building and maintaining your structures? The choice is yours, but in this world of constant change, the best practice is probably to focus on revisiting your plan on a quarterly basis and also whenever circumstances warrant.

We know that our business expert survey group "regularly" revisits these topics, but how often do they focus on these practices? These experts differ, but a plurality commit to quarterly engagements, while smaller numbers focus on annual or monthly revisits. Perhaps most telling is that very few do not revisit their business models, plans, and strategies at all, as shown in Figure 1.3.

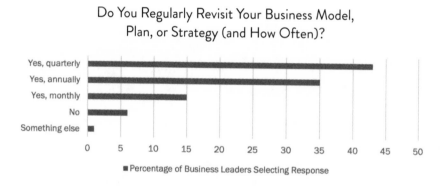

Figure 1.3

The most important takeaway from this question is that nearly 95 percent of expert business leaders revisit their business model, plans, and strategy on a regular basis. This reassessment of their core foundations validates the premise that you should focus time and energy on building and rebuilding your business.

With this context for the path forward, we now turn to the approaches, methodologies, and tools that will help you direct your energy to constructive and efficient actions.

IN REVIEW

What did we learn from this chapter?

1. You bring a personal context and personal biases to your business ventures. You should use your valuable experiences and lessons learned to be better prepared for what is ahead.

2. While acknowledging your personal context, it is important to consider a future context that involves constructive action focusing on:

   a. Building from the ground up

   b. Worrying productively

   c. Embracing change

   d. Trusting yourself and your team

   e. Making the commitment

3. Successful business leaders feel well prepared for the challenges that their businesses will face next.

Prior to detailing the approaches, methodologies, and tools you can use to help position you and your business for success, it is worth considering the four questions on the following pages. These questions will help you establish the context for your future planning based on your past experiences.

FOR FURTHER EXPLORATION

What are your most formative experiences that have led to great successes or unfortunate failures within your career or at your current business so far? What are your best lessons from those experiences?

_____

_____

_____

_____

Based on your experiences, what biases do you bring to assessment, decision-making, planning, and implementation activities? How do these biases impact those activities?

_____

_____

_____

_____

How do you currently assess, decide, plan, and implement new initiatives for your business? Do you feel like your process helps you be well prepared for the future? If not, what can you do to prepare?

_____

_____

_____

_____

How do you define success and failure for your business ventures?

_____

_____

_____

_____

2

THE BLUEPRINT

"You don't have to be a genius or a visionary or
even a college graduate to be successful. You just
need a framework and a dream."

—MICHAEL DELL

Now that we have revisited your toughest experiences, best lessons, biases, and current strategies for approaching the future of your business and have examined how to extend your personal context, it is time to leverage this work and dive into the framework that will help you build your business better and drive toward success rather than failure.

We will dive into the core approaches, methodologies, and tools that can be applied throughout all business stages—starting up, scaling up, breaking up, handing off, and others—and throughout your business career.

With this process for developing your designs and blueprints for repairing and rebuilding your business, we will rely heavily on design-thinking fundamentals with a bias for driving actions and quickly achieving outcomes. Together, the approaches, methodologies, and tools will support the following actions:

- Assessing—identifying problems and opportunities and their contexts to understand the benefits of addressing these problems and opportunities and formulating the pathways for addressing the problems and opportunities

- Deciding—selecting the pathways that produce the most benefit for the most significant problems and opportunities

- Planning—using a streamlined and manageable model

- Implementing—focusing on orderly execution

In the chapters that follow, we will apply these core building concepts to eight critical and strategic decision categories. This process will put you and your business on the best path to achieve success. The concepts in this chapter should not be viewed as applicable only to those eight categories; they should be used throughout your business career as you determine what categories of decisions will provide the most robust structures to support the future success of your business.

With this context for the path forward, let us now turn to the approaches, methodologies, and tools that will help you direct your energy to constructive and efficient actions.

Architecting Through Approaches

The process for developing designs and blueprints for repairing and rebuilding your business leverages design-thinking fundamentals with a goal of driving actions and achieving success quickly. It is a bit of a paradox that although thinking drives the ideal process, too much thinking can derail your potential and cause paralysis by analysis.

If you are prone to overthinking—and many of us are by nature—it is important to temper those habits as you design for the future. Just like worrying too much (and unproductively) is something to avoid, overemphasizing the thinking portion of the design process must be tempered too.

Let us begin by defining each term: *approaches*, *methodologies*, and *tools*. Simply put, our approaches are the overall concepts that guide our use of the methodologies and tools. Our methodologies are the steps we use to apply our approach. Our tools are the mechanisms we use to apply our methodologies. Together, approaches, methodologies, and tools provide the core elements that drive the process for architecting our structural components for building and rebuilding our business or businesses.

Approach #1:
Leveraging Human-Centered Design Thinking

The approaches that will guide your business planning and the actions you will take are rooted in traditional design thinking—specifically, human-centered design. If you are unfamiliar with design thinking, you may wonder what exactly that means and why design-thinking approaches are important to the future of your business.

But before we dive into design thinking and human-centered design, a little additional information on my background might be useful. I was born to an entrepreneurial engineer and a pragmatic psychologist, so you might imagine that human-centered design, which combines product development and human insights, would have been an obvious field of study and career path for me. Instead, after formal training as an attorney, an informal trial by fire as a start-up business leader, and a subsequent immersion in product design and management practices, I ended up as a human-centered design practitioner by accident and without any formal training.

I mention my educational trajectory only because human-centered design and design thinking occasionally can produce great outcomes when people who are self-taught focus on outcomes rather than on rigid practices. To some extent, this book provides you with a primer on how to leverage design thinking for yourself and your business. This book gives you the freedom to design the appropriate structures for the future of your business, without attempting to enforce any doctrine.

What are design thinking and human-centered design? First, it is important to note that these terms have historically been tied to actual products—software, devices, and other things—that we use. This is how the concept was described by early practitioners such as John Arnold in *Creative Engineering* and Bruce Archer in *Systematic Method for Designers* in the late 1950s and 1960s.

These concepts picked up momentum in the 1980s, 1990s, and 2000s as they began to be used not just for product design, but also for broader business applications. The concepts were used for non-product purposes, such as designing the suite of services offered by a firm or designing large organizational structures and processes. Many believe the idea really rose to prominence after a 2008 *Harvard Business Review* article titled "Design Thinking" by Tim Brown, then CEO of IDEO, one of the leading global design firms. In the article, Brown talked about the value that design thinking can bring to the business world where "most management ideas and best practices are freely available to be copied and exploited. Leaders now look to innovation as a principal source of differentiation and competitive advantage; they would do well to incorporate design thinking into all phases of the process."[3]

As the concept evolved, it became clear that the individuals who were going to use the products, engage the services, or work in the businesses were key contributors to the design-thinking practices, rather than simply the recipients of innovations. In fact, placing these humans and their insights at the center of the design-thinking process was critical to its success. With that understanding, human-centered design thinking grew to become the standard approach for innovation in business.

What does this mean for us as we think about how to build our business better? Who is the key human at the center of your business journey?

---

3   Tim Brown, "Design Thinking," *Harvard Business Review*, June 2008, https://hbr.org/2008/06/design-thinking.

Is it you? And who are the other humans who have a voice and a role in your business journey? Your team? Your partners and investors? Your advisors? Your customers? Your family?

All of these people who are important to you have critical roles to play helping us to build and rebuild our businesses. As a result, many of these individuals can and should play roles in our processes. In short, you and these individuals are the humans at the center of the design-thinking approach.

Approach #2:
Emphasizing Problems, Opportunities, and Solution Pathways

What is the focus of the approach? Is it the organization? Is it you as the executive leader?

No. Actually, it is quite simple. The approach focuses on three concepts: problems, opportunities, and solution pathways. These concepts are used during assessment, decision-making, planning, and implementation. We recommend applying these concepts to the eight critical and strategic decision categories discussed in this book, but you should apply these concepts to the critical and strategic decision categories specific to your business.

We focus on problems, opportunities, and solution pathways, because they are the only practical way to move you and your business from where you are today to a better place tomorrow. This approach is grounded in reality. Basing your planning for the future on your current position is the most certain way to actually build your dreams. After all, if you do not focus on the circumstances of today, you will not be able to craft a viable plan for tomorrow.

You may note that problems and opportunities mean we do not just focus on some idealized future state that we then try to build steps to achieve. This "current state versus future state" comparison, which I admit I fell prey to using for a long time, is a recipe for disaster. This future-centric model focuses you and your team on distant points on the horizon that you hope to reach, rather than attainable goals driven by your actual problems and solutions. Unfortunately, because the current state versus future state mentality focuses on a long-term horizon, it does not help you focus on building the incremental infrastructure that will ensure you are making the right decisions in the near term. This is why we focus on two drivers of change: problems you have and opportunities you wish to seize. These problems and opportunities may be solved or seized quickly or over a period of years, but focusing on pain points and prospects for successes drives better decisions during your journey and delivers you to an optimal future state.

The solution pathways are not necessarily solutions. Instead, they are concepts for how to reach solutions. We cannot decide how to act until we explore our options. Moreover, we cannot determine solutions until we try to implement some of them and see how our assessment, decision-making, planning, and implementation decisions play out.

Approach #3:
Never Getting Comfortable

We know that change is going to reach our business and us, so we must embrace the concept that action is unlikely to derail our business, but inaction likely will. Many businesses and business writers have noted that a "bias for action" is important. Global giant Amazon has made it one of its defining business principles.

But a bias for action is often not sufficient for small- and medium-sized businesses. We face greater threats to our businesses, our team's livelihoods, and our own incomes than larger businesses. As a board member once mentioned to me after a large software sales deal fell apart, "No one gets fired for buying software from Microsoft or IBM. They will, though, potentially get fired from buying software from your small company."

Large enterprises and the relative stickiness of their customer and supplier relationships creates an enormous amount of inertia that, unfortunately, most of our businesses do not obtain. But we do end up with another type of inertia that can kill our businesses: the inertia of our business operations.

Who among us has not gone through weeks, months, or even years without questioning the need for changing our business? It is easy to do. You get comfortable with your routine. I certainly do. We even work to create routines for our business that, although important for monitoring activities, may have the unfortunate consequence of lulling us to sleep when it comes to recognizing the need for change. Those routines, that comfort, and the associated inertia ultimately create enormous risks for our businesses, for our teams, and for us.

How do we break the cycle? It is simple. We should never get comfortable. What does this mean in practice? For me, it means always having three changes that we are focusing on as a business at any time. We may have one or two more that are prioritized as the next initiatives, but I try to stick with only three changes in action at any time. Sometimes, these changes are not major. They can be small adjustments to the team, its products or services, or the business practices.

Is three some type of magic number for change initiatives? Not really. The right number of change initiatives for you and your business should be determined by you. Three is the right number for me. It allows me to focus and actually make sure that tasks are completed and changes occur. It has been the right number for many other experts, too. For you, it might be more or less. Only you will know what is right for you and your business.

Approach #4:
Rebuilding the Foundations First

As you might have guessed, the final element of our approach is to focus on the foundational aspects of your business. We usually find that reexamination of the following eight key areas for critical and strategic decisions will drive positive business outcomes:

- Governance models and governance team composition

- Management team models, composition, engagement, and compensation

- Adjustments and pivots

- Growth and infrastructure development

- Business disputes and breakups

- Acquisitions, mergers, exits, and other business transactions

- Disaster preparedness

- Succession planning

Focusing on the foundational elements—whatever you decide they are for your business—is essential for your sustained future success. When you emphasize these core structural components, you will find that all of the other decisions you need to make become easier and your business seems to operate better.

Only you and your team know what the foundational elements of your business are or should be. You should use the methodologies and tools in this book to create the foundational layer and structural components that you need for your business or businesses.

Methodologies Overview

Now that the approaches have been explained, what methods do we use to apply them?

The methodologies are simple and direct.

The elements of the methodologies revolve around a series of considerations for each specific phase of assessing, decision-making, planning, and implementation. Combined with the approach just described, these elements will help you create a simple framework you can rely on to build strong and resilient structural components that drive your business success.

How you apply these methodologies is entirely up to you. In the chapters ahead, we will rely on these methodologies and tools to help us make the eight critical and strategic decisions needed to drive the future success of our businesses.

We begin with the basic methodologies that can be applied—likely with some minor customization—to any foundational components of your business.

Methodology #1: Assessing

When we begin assessing what changes to make in our business, the first step is to question ourselves to identify and document the problems or opportunities that exist for our business. We do this to understand why the problems are occurring, how we may be able to solve them, and identify ways to seize the opportunities. In effect, this means that we focus on the needs and the outcomes instead of idealized solutions.

We begin by asking two simple questions: What problems in our business need solving and what opportunities exist for our business? We may have few or many, but for each problem or opportunity, we need to start by answering those questions.

Next, for each problem or opportunity, we should ask one question: What is the background and context of this problem or opportunity? This question may involve some research, which is the only time I would recommend sourcing data and information from outside your team. But before you spend a single penny of your resources, you and your team should provide the best answers that you can on your own.

Then, for each problem and opportunity, we should ask three more questions:

1. How does this problem or opportunity impact us and the future success or failure of our business?

2. Are there any constraints on potential solutions to the problem or on ways to meet the opportunity and, if there are, what are they?

3. What are the expected benefits of solving the problem or meeting the opportunity?

Finally, we turn to solution pathways for each problem and opportunity and ask ourselves one question: What are the options for solving the problem or meeting the opportunity?

As you can see in Figure 2.1, this assessment offers a reasonably developed concept for solving a problem or seizing an opportunity that should be a valuable asset for you and your business. Realizing the value of this assessment will only occur if you follow the rest of the process and continue using the methodologies or similar practices.

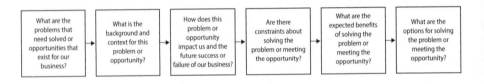

Figure 2.1. Visualization of Assessment Methodology

You may be wondering how often you should do this assessment and with whom. That is obviously up to you and your team, but the best results tend to be produced by an "always on" sourcing and curation of problems, opportunities, and solution pathways. Decision-making should be done in smaller doses and is discussed in the next section.

Methodology #2: Deciding

The methodology for approaching decision-making about the priorities for planning and implementation activities is simpler than the assessment process. Unfortunately, we have probably all experienced business phases where *everything* was a priority. As a result, *nothing* was really a priority and, in most instances, the business failed to move forward and be prepared for the future.

Businesses I have been involved with, either as an executive or advisor, that have produced the greatest successes—in terms of both sustained business success and lucrative exits for their team and stakeholders—have used models for decision-making that rely on a regular (generally quarterly) decision-making process. But they also create the opportunity for emergent decision-making based on exigent circumstances—both good and bad. This allows the business to have a regular rhythm for revisiting priorities, making decisions to embrace new changes, and scheduling deep-dive reviews of a number of the critical and strategic areas to ensure that proper time is devoted to each area on no less than an annual basis.

But the schedule for making decisions is only part of the equation. How do you identify the most significant problems and opportunities and drive the goals of your business or businesses? How should you go about selecting the potential solution pathways that may produce the most benefit for your business? How do you actually make the decisions?

Many of the businesses that I help guide have adopted a stage-gate process (with a minimum of two gates) to create and sustain success. The stage-gates are ranked according to a small number of criteria.

How does this work in practice? Figure 2.2 illustrates the simplicity of the model. Initially, you and your team agree to the criteria for the first stage-gate, which generates three outcomes: (1) initiatives for further evaluation and prioritization, (2) parking lot items for future decision-making cycles, and (3) archived concepts for future reference. Then, you and your team use a second set of objective criteria with associated points (which can be positive or negative) to score and rank the initiatives for further evaluation and prioritization. From this second set of objective criteria, you generate the rank order list that, if the process is structured correctly, guides the selection of the priorities for planning and implementation.

Great effort should be invested to ensure that this decision-making process is as efficient as possible and does not induce paralysis by analysis. For that reason, I suggest that reasonable time limitations be established by the decision-making team to set or reset the stage-gate criteria and to operate the decision-making process.

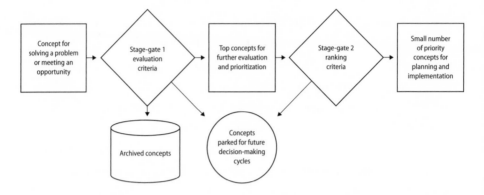

Figure 2.2. Visualization of Decision-Making Methodology

What are reasonable time limitations? Ultimately, that is up to you and your team, but in most circumstances, stage-gates can be firmly established in less than two hours, and full prioritization exercises should take no more than three hours. Otherwise, you tend to waste resources and create a sense of dread in your revenue-producing team when you need to engage in these decision processes.

Methodology #3: Planning

As simple as the decision-making methodology is in practice, the planning methodology is even more direct. Given that wasted time is wasted money, we should not plan before we have decided to act. Planning time should only be dedicated to prioritized initiatives that have been fully assessed and determined to be priorities.

But how should planning work? As you well know, it should focus on designating a leader, assembling the right team, determining the key steps for future implementation, identifying the right resources, developing the right communications strategies, and determining the reasonable timeline estimates for implementation, as depicted in Figure 2.3.

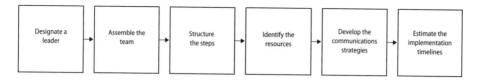

Figure 2.3. Visualization of Planning Methodology

While this is not complicated, businesses of all sizes tend to miss some of the most critical components. Sometimes the mistakes are the result of leadership by committee, while other times the issues arise because the process does not include representatives from all the parts of the business that will need to be engaged to implement the solution or that will be impacted by a change. Similarly, many times there is a failure to consider the communications that need to occur—both inside the business and outside with customers and partners—about the changes. The result is that many positive changes end up with negative perceptions.

Timing, it is often said, is everything—especially in a small- or medium-sized business. Great attention needs to be dedicated to ensuring that implementation timeline estimates are reasonable in the context of other activities while ensuring that change does not happen too slowly for the change to produce the desired outcomes as fast as possible. Speed can kill, but for most of us, acceleration fuels wins.

Methodology #4: Implementing

Assessment, decision-making, and planning are often glorified. But no function is more important for driving success and helping us steer clear of failure than implementation. One of my favorite business books is *Execution: The Discipline of Getting Things Done* by Larry Bossidy and Ram Charan.[4] I tend to never be short of ideas, but I occasionally lack the discipline to make those ideas a reality, so I have stationed multiple

---

4   Larry Bossidy and Ram Charan, *Execution: The Discipline of Getting Things Done* (New York: Crown Business, 2009).

copies of the book throughout my home and office. While this may seem odd, it is a constant reminder to me that implementation is the most critical step in the process and the one in which, unfortunately, many leaders do not actively engage. Too many of us assume that since we have invested the hard work to assess, decide, and plan, the activation of these ideas will occur because we have agreed or directed that the implementation should occur.

How many times have you seen the execution of a well-structured plan fail to succeed? Far too often, right? That is why when it is time to implement, you need to ensure that you have designated a leader for implementation, empowered the utilization of the right team members and resources, established an implementation monitoring protocol, developed a schedule for the key implementation steps, established a mechanism for identifying and managing unforeseen issues and obstacles, and determined the required final activity for implementation completion. Figure 2.4 illustrates the basic implementation methodology that can help with implementation activities to position your business ventures for success.

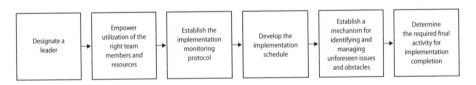

Figure 2.4. Visualization of Implementation Methodology

The Tools

The tools for managing these approaches and methodologies do not need to be glamorous. In fact, we use the simple tools provided in the pages that follow.

The first tool (Table 2.1) is used for our assessment and tracking of decision-making and should only include one problem or opportunity for each use of the tool to support clear thinking and determinations of priorities and actions.

PROBLEM AND OPPORTUNITY CARD TEMPLATE

Problem/Opportunity Title	
Problem/Opportunity Summary	
Background/Context	
Impact and Alignment to Future Success or Failure	
Constraints on Solving/Meeting	
Benefits of Solving/Meeting	
Options for Solving/Meeting	
Applicable Category	
Prioritization	
Status	

Table 2.1. Tool for Assessing and Tracking Decision-Making

DECISION-MAKING STAGE-GATES TEMPLATE

Problem/ Opportunity Title		
Stage-Gate #	Questions to Answer	Result
Stage-Gate 1	• Question 1: Does the problem or opportunity cause a loss of revenue, loss of profit margin, loss of employees, misalignment of our mission, or other potential failure? • Question 2: Does the solution represent an opportunity to increase revenue, margins, team stability, business alignment to mission, or future success? • Question 3: Does the problem or opportunity merit potential prioritization despite not eliciting a "yes" to one of the preceding questions?	If the answer is "yes" to at least two questions, the problem and opportunity card should be moved to stage-gate 2. If the answer is "yes" to only one of the first two questions but not the third question, it should be parked for future consideration. If the answer is "no" to all three questions, the problem and opportunity card should be archived for future reference.
Stage-Gate 2	• Question 1: Can the problem be solved or opportunity seized for a reasonable investment of resources and within a reasonable timeline? • Question 2: Should we prioritize the solving of the problem or the seizing of the opportunity as one of our top five priorities to position the business for success and/or avoid failure?	If the answer is "yes" to both questions, the problem and opportunity card should be moved to planning. If the answer is "yes" to only one of the first two questions, it should be parked for future consideration and planned only as time permits. If the answer is "no" to both questions, the problem and opportunity card should be archived for future reference.

Table 2.2. Default Tool for Decision-Making

The second tool (Table 2.2) is used for establishing the stage-gates for decision-making. Every business's stage-gates are different, but the ones shown in the table are the default stage-gates that have evolved over some twenty years of work. These recommendations can serve as a starting point before you develop your own.

The third tool (Table 2.3) is our initiative planning charter template, which serves as a dashboard for initiative planning. It is supported by more deeply detailed planning documents, but having this summary helps to ensure that the methodologies are followed. At this stage, we shift our language from "problem or opportunity" to "initiative" if the decision-making process has resulted in a determination to move forward and commit to action.

INITIATIVE PLANNING CHARTER TEMPLATE

Initiative Title	
Problem/Opportunity and Initiative Summary	
Planning Leader	
Planning Team Members	
Key Implementation Steps	
Resources Needed	
Communications Strategy and Steps	
Key Implementation Timelines	

Table 2.3. Initiative Planning Charter Template

The fourth tool (Table 2.4) is our initiative implementation charter template. Like the planning charter template, it serves as a dashboard for initiative implementation and, while clearly supported by more detailed implementation documents, helps to ensure that the methodologies are followed.

INITIATIVE IMPLEMENTATION CHARTER TEMPLATE

Initiative Title	
Problem/Opportunity and Initiative Summary	
Implementation Leader	
Implementation Team Members	
Implementation Resources	
Implementation Monitoring Protocol	
Key Implementation Steps and Schedule	
Issues/Obstacles Encountered and Resulting Implementation Plan Changes	
Final Activity Required for Initial Implementation Completion	

Table 2.4. Initiative Implementation Charter Template

Now you have the detailed descriptions of the context, approaches, methodologies, and tools to support you as you strengthen your business and put it on the road to success rather than the road to failure. With that foundation, it is time to begin learning how to apply these concepts to the eight critical and strategic business decision categories.

Notes about Applying the Methodologies and Tools

When you apply the methodologies and the tools, you can take one of two pathways: (1) a structured approach that uses the categories in a specific order—whatever order you determine is best for your business team—to stimulate thinking during the assessment activities or (2) a less structured approach that relies on an open discussion of problems and opportunities and then uses the categories to organize the results from your assessment exercises. Either pathway works, but if you use the less structured, open discussion approach, given the importance of the eight critical and strategic business decision categories, it is important to revisit each of the categories following your open discussion to make sure that you do not miss any of your future building blocks.

When you do explore these categories and other areas that you deem important to your business, you should, and likely will, generate many more problems and opportunities than you can advance to implementation in the near future. Since we are builders who want strong structures to support our business, we are usually not complacent, and the work of architecting and building our foundations is never done.

During the exploration of the critical and strategic categories in the chapters that follow, the tools will be used to illustrate the application of the approaches, methodologies, and tools for a fictional business that is a composite of many businesses I have helped lead or advise. The examples in each chapter will be limited to a single problem or opportunity for each of the categories. Each example will be subjected to the second stage-gate evaluation model based on the hypothetical needs of this imagined business to generate a notional prioritization for each problem or opportunity.

When you apply the approaches, methodologies, and tools, you likely will find that using the stage-gate process with our second tool will be helpful to you when determining how your multitude of business problems and opportunities should be triaged to position your business for future success. Your priorities may differ from those of the fictional business used in this book even if, magically, your problems and opportunities are identical.

Before we dive into the eight categories, we will look at the reasons that businesses fail. After all, we should learn from failures—whether our own or those of others. But first we will review the topics in this chapter and give you the opportunity to explore your thoughts on some of the concepts.

IN REVIEW

What did we learn from this chapter?

1. The approaches, methodologies, and tools that can position you for success are:

    a. Assessing—identifying problems and opportunities and their contexts to understand the benefits of addressing these problems and opportunities, and formulating the pathways for addressing the problems and opportunities

    b. Deciding—selecting the pathways that produce the most benefit for the most significant problems and opportunities

    c. Planning—using a streamlined and manageable model

    d. Implementing—focusing on orderly execution

2. The approaches focus on:

    a. Leveraging human-centered design thinking

    b. Emphasizing problems, opportunities, and solution pathways

   c. Never getting comfortable

   d. Rebuilding the foundations first

3. The methodologies for each specific phase of assessing, decision-making, planning, and implementation revolve around a series of considerations that will help you create a simple framework for architecting strong and resilient structural components that will drive your business success.

Now that you understand the approaches, methodologies, and tools, it is time to explore four questions below, which are aligned to the information in this chapter. These questions will help you determine how to properly build and rebuild the internal foundations of your business.

FOR FURTHER EXPLORATION

What do you believe to be the key foundational elements of your business?

_____

_____

_____

_____

What foundational elements of your business need the most rebuilding attention?

_____

_____

_____

_____

What have you done to date to prepare for these rebuilds to chart a course for success?

_____

_____

_____

_____

How could you begin to adopt the approaches, methodologies, and tools discussed in this chapter to support your business?

_____

_____

_____

_____

3

LEARNING FROM FAILURE

"Failure is a great teacher and, if you are open to it,
every mistake has a lesson to offer."

—OPRAH WINFREY

Before we start exploring the application of the framework's approaches, methodologies, and tools to the eight critical and strategic decision categories, it is important to explore why we focus on these specific areas. These eight critical and strategic decision categories are key elements that produce success, but these areas are also the root causes of nearly all business failures.

As many have written, and as all of us who run businesses have heard more times than we would like, the vast majority of small businesses fail. As a result, most business leaders worry about failure. In fact, the fear of failure, as noted by *Inc.* magazine in a 2022 survey of their *Inc.* 5000 companies, is the most significant struggle for 46 percent of small- and medium-sized business leaders. This worry beat all other worries by more than double digits.[5] Studying failure is not uplifting, but it does provide us

---

5   "Portrait of the American Entrepreneur by the Numbers," *Inc.*, September 2022, 64.

with valuable lessons on what not to do. As a result, it may help us manage some of our worries.

In the United States, based on survey data from the U.S. Bureau of Labor Statistics[6] that has been repeatedly cited or validated by myriad other parties,[7] American businesses and their failure rates follow a standard pattern:

- Approximately 20 percent of businesses fail in their first year after launch.

- Roughly 30 percent of businesses fail by their second year of operations.

- A staggering 50 percent of businesses fail by their fifth year of operations.

- A frightening total of almost 70 percent of businesses fail by their tenth year of operations.

But why do businesses fail?

If you have ever suffered a business failure or near-failure, you undoubtedly know exactly why that business failed. Maybe it was one reason, or maybe it was multiple reasons. Either way, you know why, and you likely suffered as a result of it—financially, emotionally, and in other ways.

In most instances, and with hindsight, you have probably surmised that these struggles were preventable or could have been avoided in some way. Maybe you should have read more, consulted a peer, or planned better. If you have done a little digging or talked with other fellow business leaders, you have probably found someone else who faced the same problems you experienced.

Because business failures and business struggles are all too prevalent, it

---

6   Bureau of Labor Statistics, Business Employment Dynamics, http://bls.gov/bdm.

7   Small Business Administration, "Small Business Facts: Do economic or industry factors affect business survival?," https://www.sba.gov/sites/default/files/Business-Survival.pdf.

is worth looking at why businesses face these difficulties. Understanding the "why" will help position you to build better businesses that succeed rather than fail. We will develop this understanding by looking at the results of the survey of successful leaders of small- and medium-sized businesses that we conducted to support this book.

What Do Successful Business Leaders Say about Failure?

Turning back to this survey, we will look at what these leaders told us about their difficulties during their business ventures. Not surprisingly, most of the leaders we surveyed track the general statistics of business failures and near failures. Their insights validate the idea that we share common problems, and that core approaches, methodologies, and tools can be successfully applied throughout all stages—starting up, scaling up, breaking up, handing off, and so on—of your business journey and business career.

Many of the business leaders we surveyed did not have a business actually fail and dissolve. But for those who did, the top five causes were the following issues:

1. Disputes between co-owners

2. Failure to pivot the business model

3. Failure to execute on a planned merger, acquisition, or sale of the business

4. Failure to build internal infrastructure to support growth

5. Failure to respond to difficulties or disasters

These reasons probably sound quite familiar. And they probably resonate with us when we examine our own common experiences and those of our peers. Note that all of these reasons align with one of our eight critical and strategic decision categories.

Given these top five drivers of business failures, it is also worth examining the most difficult phase these expert leaders experienced in their business careers, whether the troubles led to a failure or not. Although the responses to this question may have been skewed, in part, by the fact that the survey was conducted during the COVID-19 pandemic, we found remarkable consistency in the responses. The business leaders said that the most difficult phase of their business career was facing an emerging difficulty or disaster (including the COVID-19 pandemic, the Great Recession, new government policies, or disruptive competition).

Other difficult phases for these business leaders were pivoting the business model, the initial start-up phase, building or restructuring the management team, conflict with business partners, and business transactions (such as a sale of a business, a merger, or an acquisition). Each of these causes mustered the support of at least 5 percent of the respondents.

The complete results for this survey question are shown in Figure 3.1.

What Has Been Your Most Difficult Business Phase?

Figure 3.1

When I reflect on the most difficult phases of my business experiences, the most difficult phase of each business success—and what triggered each business failure—was pivoting the business model or failing to pivot the business model. Many of the successful and attempted pivots with which I have personally been involved are detailed in Chapter 6. I have little doubt that, despite experiencing strong business headwinds during the COVID-19 pandemic and the Great Recession, pivots have been the most stressful, exhausting, and (in many ways) rewarding business phases. I certainly did not expect that an environmental commodity trading software platform company was going to need to transform itself into a software development tools company before finally finding its path to success as an early mover Internet of Things software company. The opportunity for success sometimes involves listening to your customers, your team, and market opportunities rather than sticking with what you have always done or what you hoped to do.

Now for some soul searching. Looking back on your business journey, what has been your most difficult phase? What did you learn from it? We will explore your experiences in greater depth at the end of this chapter, but it may be useful to keep these troubling phases in mind as we study the difficulties and failures of others.

What can we conclude from this part of our survey? We can conclude that the most difficult phases of the business journey are all addressable in some way—so long as you use an organized approach to making key critical and strategic decisions.

That is the beauty of understanding the difficulties you will face and being ready to take on these challenges through an organized approach and evergreen tools. You will be ready. Or at least you *can* be ready.

Mistakes Were Made . . .

Although studying the difficulties that were successfully overcome may be educational, it may not be as informative as studying the mistakes that were made by the business leaders we surveyed. While we remember the challenges we have faced, the mistakes we have made are what we vow never to repeat. And the mistakes are usually easier to learn how to avoid, even when based on the mistakes of others. After all, mistakes involve choices, whereas difficulties may be thrust upon us.

The business leaders we surveyed also provided informative assessments of the mistakes they made during their business careers. The four most common mistakes identified by the business leaders were not building a strong management team or not building the "right" management team, picking the "wrong" business partners, selecting the "wrong" business model, and not being able to pivot a business model. Slightly smaller numbers of business leaders indicated they had made mistakes involving exits, mergers, acquisitions, succession planning, and responses to disasters. The complete set of responses is provided in Figure 3.2.

The most difficult phases of my business life align strongly with the responses of these leaders. My Achilles' heel in business has been not building the right management team. This failing has often caused me to attempt to simultaneously juggle too many roles and struggle with the resulting workload. I am sure that many of you have experienced similar situations. As noted earlier, the single most trying issue for me in terms of management team composition has been my shortcomings as a sales leader and my inability to find strong sales leaders for the management teams I have led. This likely limited growth of each business and may have undermined the potential success of the businesses.

But what about you? What mistakes have you made in your business career? Are you like me? Do you keep making the same mistakes? Or have you been able to learn from your mistakes (and not make the same ones again)?

While I was drafting this book, I began to wonder whether these reasons for failure had been as constant over time as they seemed to be when I compared my twenty years of experience to the results of the survey of business leaders. Was this era different?

Figure 3.2

Failures of the 1960s and 1980s

Given this question, it seemed important to consider whether we were examining a unique era after the Great Recession and during the COVID-19 pandemic, which might have impacted the results of the study and my own track record. An interesting article, "Causes of New Venture Failure: 1960s vs. 1980s," by two Santa Clara University professors, Albert Bruno and Joel Leidecker, seems to indicate that nothing much had really changed between the 1960s and 1980s.[8] Not much seems to have changed between the 1960s and the 2020s, either. When comparing their analysis to the data we examined in 2020, the reasons for business failures were not that different.

Their study focused primarily on technology businesses, and they aligned the results with a product-centric view. The results of their study indicated that the principal reasons for failure were the following:

---

8   Albert V. Bruno and Joel K. Leidecker, "Causes of New Venture Failure: 1960s vs. 1980s," *Business Horizons*, Volume 31, Issue 6, November–December 1988, 51–56.

- Product timing

- Product design

- Inappropriate distribution or selling strategy

- Unclear business definition

- Overreliance on one customer

- Initial undercapitalization

- Assuming a debt instrument too early

- Problems with the venture capital relationship

- Ineffective team

- Personal problems

- One-track thinking

- Cultural/social factors[9]

Although these researchers used different terminology than our survey, the reasons cited for business troubles are aligned with the majority of our eight critical and strategic decision categories. Only two of our elements are not referenced: (1) governance models and governance team composition and (2) mergers, acquisitions, exits, and other business transactions.

Management team models, composition, engagement, and compensation were implicated in two of the reasons cited by the study: "ineffective team" and "cultural/social factors." Pivots and adjustments were aligned to four issues: "one-track thinking," "product timing," "product design," and "unclear business definition."

Growth and infrastructure development and business disputes (and breakups) map to "inappropriate distribution or selling strategy"

9   Bruno and Leidecker, "Causes of New Venture Failure: 1960s vs. 1980s," 54–56.

and "problems with the venture capital relationship" respectively. Similarly, we can compartmentalize "initial undercapitalization" and "assuming a debt instrument too early" in our disaster preparedness and management category and "personal problems" within our succession planning category.

What can we conclude from this study? Simply put, this study that analyzes the reasons for failures from up to and over half a century ago delivers roughly the same outcomes—albeit in different words—for business failures. Does that not strike you as absolutely insane?

Why Do We Repeat History?

Despite all of our technological advances, tools for monitoring business performance, and self-actualization approaches, the reasons our businesses fail today (and have failed during the past decade) are aligned with the same drivers of business troubles from more than fifty years ago.

We simply have not figured out how to focus on setting the right structures in place for sustained business success. Maybe, just maybe, it is time to take a disciplined approach using a simple framework for assessing, determining, planning, and implementing decisions about key structural components of our business. As radical as this may sound, this opportunity has been right in front of us for a long time.

From their survey, Bruno and Leidecker drew a number of conclusions about business failures, all of which add credence to the need for the framework offered in this book. Some of their conclusions are particularly relevant: "Failure is a process that occurs over time," failure is caused by "specific identifiable factors," and identifying these factors "can lead to steps intended to avoid or prevent failure."[10]

While the conclusions from Bruno and Leidecker remain true today, their conclusion that "knowledge of the presence of these factors can lead to steps intended to avoid or prevent failure" is particularly significant. This conclusion highlights the need to focus on benefiting from the

---

10   Bruno and Leidecker, "Causes of New Venture Failure: 1960s vs. 1980s," 52.

lessons learned from the mistakes and failures of the past when building businesses. Unfortunately, we business leaders seem to be better at spotting mistakes in the rearview mirror than through our windshields, no matter how often the mistakes are repeated by us and our peers.

Why is it, then, that we fail or trend toward failure for the same reasons business leaders did in the 1960s and 1980s? Most likely it is because we are so focused on trying to operate our businesses (and survive) that we fail to take the time to systematically assess, make decisions, plan, and implement for the critical and strategic activities that allow us and our businesses to avoid failure.

That was certainly true for me historically, as my business partners, investors, and teammates in those businesses likely would tell you. The biggest stumbling blocks I have encountered in the business ventures in which I have had a leadership role echo the causes cited in this chapter:

- Not having the right personal psychological makeup to drive sales

- Not having a balanced board of directors with diverse experiences to support business strategy development

- Not having the right team composition and balance to meet the need to increase sales and operate the business

- Not having the right product, business model, or sales model

- Not being ready for disasters (including the Great Recession, the COVID-19 pandemic, and losing large customers)

- Not having built enough internal infrastructure to maintain and support growth

I discuss these and other obstacles that I have personally experienced in depth in subsequent chapters. I have found ways to overcome nearly all of them by using a disciplined approach to assess, determine, plan, and implement decisions.

The obstacles I have encountered and the mistakes I have made have led to one conclusion: There is a better way to approach the potential problems a business may face and to seize the opportunities that may fuel growth.

The Challenges Ahead

Now you are armed with the insights from the expert business leaders who have had the benefit of rearview mirror visibility. But before we start looking at the future of your business, we will look at some of the insights these expert leaders had about the challenges they saw on the horizon.

We asked the business leaders this question: What do you think is the most challenging period or activity your business will face in the next five to ten years? The business leaders indicated that their most common concerns were exiting their business through a sale of their business or leadership succession, pivoting their business model, or mergers and acquisitions. Other concerns—including the uncertain and unknown, internal business conflicts, and disasters—were less frequently identified as challenges. The full results from this survey question are shown in Figure 3.3.

What Will Be the Most Challenging Future Issues for Your Business?

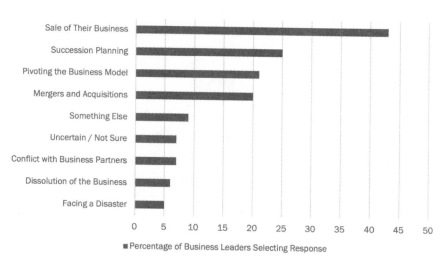

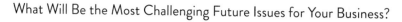

Figure 3.3

What can we learn from this? Probably the most valuable lesson is that even highly successful business leaders who are viewed as experts by their peers know that there are future challenges in front of them.

In this survey, many of their challenges were about exiting the business—either selling the business or handling succession planning—but many were impacted by the need to pivot their business model again. This challenge of pivoting was, as you may recall, also one of their most difficult challenges in the past.

When I look at the challenges that are in front of me and the business I lead, the most challenging issues for me are aligned with these results—it is where the story ends and trying to make the best ending possible. Maybe that will require a pivot, a merger, or an acquisition (or multiple acquisitions). Maybe it will be an exit—through a sale of the business, the transfer of executive leadership roles through succession, or something else. Whatever the future holds, I am certain it will hold challenges, and I am also certain I need to be prepared for these obstacles and opportunities.

What about you and your business—or businesses? What future challenges will you face?

No one has all of the foresight, strategies, and plans that will guarantee challenges will not arise. We are not alone, but we can be more prepared.

Ready?

Are you ready for what is next for your business? Maybe?

Even many of the experts we surveyed indicated that, despite their decades of experience and great successes in business, they were not sure whether they were ready for the challenges their businesses would face. When asked whether they were ready for what their business would face in the years ahead, nearly all the business leaders responded in the affirmative, although more than 40 percent indicated that they were less ready for potentially unforeseen events. The full results are shown in Figure 3.4.

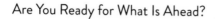

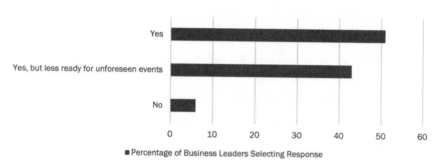

Figure 3.4

Why are they ready? The same reason that I feel like I am ready. Quite simply—they do the challenging work with a disciplined approach for assessing, determining, planning, and implementing decisions about key structural components of their business. This is evident from their clarity on their past challenges, analysis of their prior mistakes, their grasp of the challenges that are ahead of them, and their unwavering belief in their readiness for what lies ahead.

It is time to get ready for what is next for your business—just like the experts we surveyed.

What Positions Us for Success?

For us—like these leaders—the pathway to success is found through executing a disciplined approach to assessing, determining, planning, and implementing decisions about key structural components of our business. After all, we have seen from the survey of these leaders and the Bruno and Leidecker assessment that failure is most often caused by not following a disciplined approach and by a lack of focus on the right internal factors.

You should ultimately create your own list of the most important decisions you need to emphasize for you and your business, but the eight critical and strategic decision categories are a great starting point—and this is where I stay focused. Two of these categories focus on your team—both governance and management teams. The next two categories focus on your core business activities—adjustments or pivots and internal infrastructure for growth. Two more categories look at ownership changes—both business breakups (or disputes) and combinations (mergers, acquisitions, exits, or other business transactions). The last two categories focus on managing uncertainties—disasters and succession.

All of these decisions impact your business at all stages of maturity. Given how the odds are so stacked against business success, it is important to address each one early and revisit often.

Before we turn to a tutorial on the core approaches, methodologies, and tools that you can apply throughout all stages of your business journey and business career to help position you for success, it is important to do a little reflection.

IN REVIEW

What did we learn from this chapter?

1. Nearly all business leaders view a limited number of internal decision categories as critical to the success (or failure) of their business:

    a. Governance models and governance team composition

    b. Management team models, composition, engagement, and compensation

    c. Adjustments and pivots

    d. Growth and infrastructure development

    e. Business disputes and breakups

    f. Acquisitions, mergers, exits, and other business transactions

    g. Disaster preparedness and management

    h. Succession planning

2. Your past experiences can color your future, but they do not determine it. Learn from the mistakes you have made so you can be better prepared for what is ahead.

3. Successful business leaders feel well prepared for the challenges their businesses will face next.

Now that we have explored the reasons for business failures over time in this chapter, it is time to contemplate four questions on the following pages. These questions will help guide your future assessment, decision-making, planning, and implementation based on your past experiences with failures and difficult times.

FOR FURTHER EXPLORATION

What are the major reasons you experienced business difficulties or business failures within your career and ventures?

_____

_____

_____

_____

How have you changed your approach to building or rebuilding your business ventures based on those experiences?

_____

_____

_____

_____

What are the most significant future challenges you believe you and your business ventures will face?

_____

_____

_____

_____

What are you doing now to be ready for these future challenges and associated opportunities?

_____

_____

_____

_____

4

YOUR SECURITY COUNCIL

"If I have seen further, it is by
standing on the shoulders of giants."

—ISAAC NEWTON

You and your commitment. You and your energy. You and your desire to succeed. You and your refusal to fail. Your business, your team, your family, and your customers probably rely on you—perhaps to a fault.

You have paid, and likely continue to pay, a steep price in the form of feeling overwhelmed, stress-induced insomnia, sleepless nights of work or worry, missed time with family and friends, and feeling alone on an island of self-doubt and worry.

Who helps set the direction of your business, monitors the execution of these strategies, and revisits the direction? Do you have a formal team—including outside experts—that helps you with these activities? If so, you are ahead of most of your small- and medium-sized business leader peers. Or do you or you and your business partners do these roles exclusively?

You need not go it alone. Nor do you and your business partner or partners need to continue to suffer from one-on-one jousting matches over strategies and initiatives. There is much to gain from engaging other experts with leadership experience in your business venture.

In basketball, there is a saying that "hero ball" does not win. The concept of hero ball is rooted in the theory that the best player on the team can personally "will" the group to victory by taking shot after shot since, after all, this individual is the best player. It seems to have worked for Michael Jordan, so it should work for the best player on any basketball team. Right? Wrong. In fact, Michael Jordan was as successful as he was, in part, because of Scottie Pippen and other teammates who constantly played off of and fed the ball to Jordan. If the concept of hero ball does not even apply to Michael Jordan, it is unlikely to be a great concept for basketball games or business activities. Sure, this approach might win a game or two, but it does not win basketball championships. And as you can gather, it does not create sustained successes in business either.

The odds simply are not in favor of one talented basketball player creating win after win as a solo effort. The same is true in business. Worse still, hero ball only compounds the pressure on you and adds to the stress and risks that you and your business face.

Limiting the use of hero ball as a model of practice in your business should not stop with your business partners, your management team, or your team members. What you really need are individuals on your governance team who have experience and expertise that you might not be able to hire as full-time team members. They can help you elevate your game and play at the business equivalent of championship-caliber performance.

This resource—which I loosely refer to as your security council (as a nod to the United Nations body of the same name)—should, like its global namesake, focus on the security, stability, and future of your business. This group is your governance model, and the experts you select to assist you are your governance team. The form of this security council and its composition are your choice. To make the right choice for you and your business, you can use our approaches, methodologies, and tools. Before showing you how to use the methodologies and tools to create your extended team of experts to help you stop playing hero ball, we will spend a little time looking at some of the contexts for your decisions. We will explore your governance structure options, operational models, and team composition to help you create your security council for your business.

Governance Structure Options

The term *governance* for a business likely conjures images of large publicly traded companies with boardrooms filled with large numbers of directors who can be made to support reasonable outcomes and discussions about Sarbanes-Oxley compliance, financial audit report analysis, and the like. Governance, however, does not need to involve a board of directors—or even a board of any kind. It certainly does not need to involve a large number of individuals, nor does it have to have some of the compliance and audit requirements of public company boards. Governance structures—or at a minimum, some type of advisory structure that supports your own self-governance—can take on many forms. Before we look at the governance and advisory options for you and your business ventures, we should consider why U.S. publicly traded companies have boards of directors. (It is not only due to state legal requirements that corporations have such boards.) We will also look at why other closely held businesses opt to use some type of formal governance structure.

Why is business governance important, and how does it help a business? All forms of business governance should provide a structure and the processes to help manage and guide a business. The business governance framework—integrated with the management team—should help set the direction of the company, monitor the execution of these strategies, and revisit the direction. As a result, governance should be important to you because it impacts you, your business partners, your family, your team members, your customers, and your other stakeholders.

What are the options for business governance frameworks? We have a range of choices (including many that you already know), from more formal to less formal to the hero ball model, which you may be using today. Business governance frameworks include the following:

- Board of directors—Legally defined formal group of elected individuals with the power to set business policies for management and oversight, which may also be legally required. The group may be legally defined through bylaws for a corporation, an operating agreement for a limited liability company, or a partnership agreement for a partnership.

- Advisory board—Informal body of experts and advisors that is generally not legally defined, constituted, or empowered but rather is selected, constituted, and operated by the executives and management team to provide strategic advice. The advisory board may have a formalized structure without management or oversight authority.

- Professional advisor team—Group of professionals with specific expertise, such as legal, accounting, risk management, et cetera, who serve as strategic advisors to executive management and/or a board. The professionals do not have any specific legal authority, and the group may or may not have a formalized structure.

- Friends and family council—Group of friends and family members responsible for providing strategic advice without any specific legal authority. The group may or may not have a formalized structure.

- Hero ball—The power of the one or two self-appointed "decider" or "deciders."

These governance structural options are not mutually exclusive. You can use all or even some of these options together. What is important is to determine the type of structure you wish to use to truly govern your business venture—what structure you will use to establish the direction and monitor the direction of your business. It is also important to determine how much input you want to receive from and what authority you are willing to cede to individuals who are not you or your business co-owners. The size of whatever option you select for your security council—which for most small- to medium-sized businesses should be more than two and less than eight individuals—should balance providing diversity in viewpoints and supporting collaborative dialogues that generate action.

The choice, ultimately, is yours, unless it has been determined through your legal structure or by investors in your business venture. You and your business partners likely will know the best model and size, but hero ball—or going it alone—is unlikely to be the answer that will position you for success over time.

In businesses that I have founded and led that proved to be successful—either through long-term sustained operations or an eventual acquisition by a market leader in the space we were attempting to disrupt, we used a formalized governance structure with a board of directors that was empowered to set the business policies for management and oversight. Sometimes this was required by the investors. Other times, it was based on an acknowledgment that the management team—even if they occupied a majority of seats on the board of directors—needed outside perspectives and diverse opinions to help guide the business venture. Admittedly, on the business ventures I led that failed—and there are, sadly, a few—I did not follow this process of establishing a formal structure with outside participants in the governance process. In these situations, either I or my business partners and I were left to our own instincts and biases. More often than not, this produced outcomes that were not optimal by any measure. Would the outcomes of these failures have been changed if I had used a more formal structure? Unfortunately, we will never know. But, based on my personal sample, I will not make that same mistake again.

Is my experience representative? For comparison, we will turn back to our survey. How does this group of expert business leaders approach governance? As shown in Figure 4.1, nearly 90 percent of these business leaders use some type of governance or advisory structure, and the majority—more than 60 percent—rely on a formal board of directors.

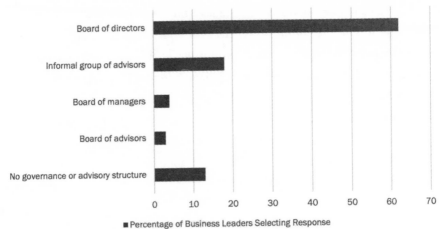

Figure 4.1

Why do these expert business leaders—and why should you—choose to have some type of additional engagement from others to support the governance of the business?

Perhaps you and your business partners, if you have them, have decided that you need objective opinions from third parties when making critical and strategic business decisions. Maybe you recognize that you have strengths and weaknesses and that board members or advisors with their own strengths can offset your weaknesses and help you make your business more successful. It could be that a governance structure is legally required. Or you may have decided that you need a broader network to help your business sales and growth activities than you or your team of business partners and employees can provide. Or could it be that you have decided that hero ball just does not work very well?

No matter the reason, it is important to decide on the model or models that are best for you and provide you with the most comfort. Once you make that decision, you will need to do some additional work to frame the model. To frame the model, you may wish to consider whether legal changes—for instance, through amendments to bylaws for a corporation or an amended and restated operating agreement for a limited liability company—are needed. Such changes would be required for a board of directors governance model. In any scenario, even if it is not legally required, it is important to create a short, concise charter that will provide the foundation for the operations of whatever governance model you choose to use. This charter will assist and protect you, your business, and the governance team members you engage. Further, this charter can be used to help generate an equally important document—a written agreement that covers the governance relationship for the third parties you engage.

Governance Operations

Now that we have examined the structural options for governance, it is important to consider the operational model for your governance structure. Operations can be logically divided into two components: content and processes.

Content for Your Governance Team

When you think about content for the governance team, what are the topics your governance team should consider during your activities, regardless of the specific structure used?

As you might guess, based on our research, the following eight critical and strategic business decision categories, which are stated in abbreviated forms, should play a role:

- Governance structure and team

- Management team and compensation

- Adjustments and pivots

- Growth and infrastructure development

- Business disputes and breakups

- Acquisitions, mergers, exits, and other business transactions

- Disaster preparedness

- Succession planning

In addition to these topics, it is also important to ensure that your governance team has the right context and information to help and advise you in making these critical and strategic decisions. For instance, you may want to provide:

- Financial reports

- Sales and marketing updates

- Market trend information

- Technology trend information

- Corporate best practices of peers or aspirational companies

- Legal, regulatory, and compliance issues

In terms of how to cover these topics, there is no perfect model. You can choose how to visit each topic, how often to address each topic, and how to determine when actions are required to address each topic, but it is important to consider these questions as you examine the processes for governance operations.

Governance Team Processes—Meetings and Beyond

Regardless of the governance structure you select, as you move from content to processes, it is important to determine how you plan to approach formal and informal meetings, communicate your expectations for engagement outside of those meetings, and provide clear expectations for your governance team members.

Public company boards of directors tend to have the ultra-formal and highly time-consuming approach of holding monthly board of directors' meetings and having multiple committees. This is largely based on their bylaws, charters, and other requirements. The committees are composed of subsets of the board and convene on a regular basis. Given the high risks of public company boards and their role as stewards of investments from individuals, retirement funds, and others, these approaches are not only logical but necessary.

What does your company need in terms of the formality and rhythm of governance operations? You probably need some type of formalized meeting schedule that balances your need for outside perspectives and decision support with being considerate of people's time—the time of the outside participants in your process, your time, and the time of your management team. You will have to balance the time needed to prepare for these meetings with the value you receive from the meetings. You should also make sure to develop the process for engagement and communications in an ad hoc manner outside of your formal meeting schedule.

What does this mean for most companies like those we operate? Based on the companies I have worked with and those that I have operated, a reasonable approach is to set quarterly meetings that are conducted virtually, with in-person attendance as an option. The meetings should be held on mutually agreeable dates and times for the governance team participants with the caveat that the executives can request special meetings or consultations when circumstances merit.

In addition, you likely will want to come to a consensus on how to transmit information in a way that allows your governance team to help you without overwhelming them with a bombardment of emails or an "always on" requirement. You can do this by using a group collaboration messaging tool. A reasonable compromise for communications is to establish a regular process for transmitting information before regular meetings, special meetings, or informal calls with sufficient advance delivery to support a review of the materials to facilitate informed conversations. You can reserve other communications unrelated to meetings and calls for urgent circumstances.

Finally, you should develop clear expectations on the time commitments you will need from your governance team members based on the processes you establish. This will allow you to articulate those expectations to candidates, which will help ensure you have the best experience and can keep strong governance team members engaged for the long haul.

How does this guidance translate to a governance operational model—especially if you want something informal rather than the formal and strong board of directors model? As an illustration, I had the honor of being asked to participate—as an advisory board of one—to support two business partners in a small industrial services company several years ago. When they approached me, the co-owners indicated they were seeking someone who could help them make strategic decisions about their business. They wanted to stop playing hero ball. They did not want someone to actually make the decisions for them; they were still the owners. But they wanted someone with an independent view to help them make their decisions and present possible alternative points of view or support one perspective over another. My only role was to be a sounding board and provider of advice. I participated in quarterly meetings and received a reasonable remuneration in return. It was simple enough for me to do, and it was a simple framework that helped the co-founders stop playing hero ball. This was a fantastic way to embrace governance structures without sacrificing control.

Why did these co-founders select me to participate in their governance activities? Probably because I fit the profile of their perceived need for an advisor, as I had served as an executive and advisor to other successful small businesses in heavily regulated industries. This brings us to our final governance component—the profiles of the members of your security council.

Governance Profile

With governance structure options and operations addressed, the last element for us to consider in your governance model are the profiles of your advisors. Think about the backgrounds and previous experience that your governance team members should possess to bring you the experience and knowledge you need to position your business for success.

In most cases, the backgrounds and roles you need from your governance team members are driven by your need for additional expertise and perspectives to complement your own capabilities and biases and those of your business partners and management team. As a result, to determine the profile of your governance team, one of the best activities you can do is to look at the eight critical and strategic decision areas and the additional context areas to assess where you need additional support.

In my first start-up experience, Augusta Systems Inc. evolved into an early Internet of Things software company that was backed by venture capital. We were a corporation, and under our bylaws we had a board of directors. But we did not build out the board outside of the co-founders until after we secured venture capital investments and an expansion of the board membership was required by the terms of the investment agreements. The investment agreements, which were fairly typical, required a five-member board consisting of two representatives of the venture investors, two management team members, and a third independent member. As a result, we needed to determine the optimal profile for that independent board member since we had only one position to use to expand our executive-level capabilities.

Since the founding team had no experience with software sales, scaling infrastructure for a venture-backed software company, or navigating to a successful exit of a venture-backed software company, the gap we needed to fill in terms of experience and expertise was clear.

The four board members—investors and management—considered their personal connections and reasonable degrees of separation to identify potential independent board member candidates who might help our management team fill the identified gaps. After discussing our options, we reached a consensus on the target—a former venture capital executive who, prior to serving as a venture investor, had led software sales for a technology company that had generated enough growth to become a publicly traded company on the NASDAQ stock exchange. After some conversations, we collaboratively created a compensation model that included some stock options and financial considerations and added her to our company board.

She was an amazing mentor for a start-up software company CEO with aspirations to build a successful business. She was more than we had hoped for because she filled the gaps we needed and was the right fit for our team. With her guidance, we were able to scale our software sales channels through global market leaders (with whom she had strong business relationships), position direct sales growth activities, and navigate the market to reach a successful exit. The exit was achieved by integrating the team and technologies into a firm, Hexagon AB, that was a global technology market leader in sensors, software, and autonomous solutions.

The same process will work for each and every potential form of your governance team or teams, including boards of directors, boards of advisors, professional advisor teams, or friends and family councils. Identify your needs, identify your candidates, examine the potential fit between the candidates and the needs, and then engage them.

If the right way to create a governance team is to align your needs for supplemental capabilities to candidates with those attributes and the right mindset for you and your business, then what is the wrong way?

The two biggest mistakes that business leaders and companies can make when selecting governance team members are (1) focusing on high-powered names for governance team roles instead of needs and alignment and (2) not including diverse experiences, perspectives, and points of view (which happens when these needs are not well-examined during the assessment phase).

This brings us to the importance of the assessment phase. We will now take a look at how to operate the process of assessing, deciding, planning, and implementing our critical and strategic decisions about our governance structure and team with an example demonstrating how to apply our tools, starting with the blueprint.

PROBLEM AND OPPORTUNITY CARD—GOVERNANCE EXAMPLE

Problem/Opportunity Title	Governance Structure and Team
Problem/Opportunity Summary	Our ownership/executive team needs additional governance team member(s) to assist us with arbitrating between potentially differing views on business strategy, providing additional perspectives, and opening doors for new direct and channel revenue opportunities.
Background/Context	Our business is struggling to grow. We have been profitable, but we have not had as much revenue growth for the past two years. Our founding team may need support to adjust our business model and connections for new sales.
Impact and Alignment to Future Success or Failure	Ideally, the new governance team member(s) would be able to provide new ideas on the business model and new introductions for sales, which will help us move from a good business to a great business.
Constraints on Solving/Meeting	The ownership team does not want to sacrifice control, so we only want to have an advisory board to support governance and not an expansion of our board of directors.
Benefits of Solving/Meeting	We might be able to increase our growth and ensure that our business leaders do not grow frustrated with one another with growth stagnant.
Options for Solving/Meeting	Develop a board of advisors—initially of no more than three members—to support governance. Each individual should possess an understanding of our business industry and possess potential sales contacts, with some modest consulting payments and a small amount of stock options as compensation to align interests between the advisors and our company.
Applicable Category	Governance
Prioritization	Medium—subject to decision-making process
Status	Awaiting decision-making about prioritization

Table 4.1. Problem and Opportunity Card—Governance Example

Applying the Blueprint

Let us look at the way we would apply our methodologies and tools to examine our first critical and strategic decision question: How should I build my governance structure and team to meet my business goals without risking my culture, current freedoms, and successful trajectory?

In this example of applying our methodologies and tools from our blueprint to this question, we will use a fictional illustrative example that is a composite of a number of companies with which I have been involved. Bear in mind that you likely will generate more than one card when you advance your process, and the concept we present in Figure 4.1 is just one example to support your own process.

To help us examine governance, let us start our assessment phase by exploring the governance problems or governance opportunities that exist for our business. This likely involves an assessment of the governance structures, governance team topical knowledge and capabilities (and gaps), and individuals engaged in the governance activities of the business. Then, for each problem or opportunity, we ask the detailed questions related to background and context, impact on future success or failure, constraints on solving the problem or meeting the opportunity, expected benefits from solving the problem or meeting the opportunity, and options for solving the problem or meeting the opportunity. An example of this assessment phase for exploring potential governance improvements to create the conditions for success based on our fictional company is shown in Table 4.1.

After the assessment phase, we move from analysis and conceptualization to decision-making and, for governance, decisions about governance structures and governance team candidates.

Following our method, we recommend a simple two-step, stage-gate process to determine initiatives for further evaluation and prioritization, parking lot items for future decision-making cycles, and archived concepts for future reference. Using our standard criteria, we take our problem and opportunity card example from Table 4.1 and apply the objective criteria to guide selection of the priorities for planning and implementation with the example in Table 4.2.

DECISION-MAKING STAGE-GATES—GOVERNANCE EXAMPLE

Problem/ Opportunity Title	Governance Structure and Team	
Stage-Gate #	Questions to Answer	Result
Stage-Gate 1	• Question 1: Does the problem or opportunity cause a loss of revenue, loss of profit margin, loss of employees, misalignment of our mission, or other potential failure? • Answer 1: Yes. We lack revenue growth success and clearly need assistance to stimulate growth. • Question 2: Does the solution represent an opportunity to increase revenue, margins, team stability, business alignment to mission, or future success? • Answer 2: Yes. New advisors should be able to assist with revenue growth and maybe overall strategy to assist in future success. • Question 3: Does the problem or opportunity merit potential prioritization despite not eliciting a "yes" to one of the preceding questions? • Answer 3: Not applicable, as the answers to both Question 1 and Question 2 are "yes."	Since the answer is "yes" to the first two questions, the problem and opportunity card will be moved to decision-making stage-gate 2.
Stage-Gate 2	• Question 1: Can the problem be solved or opportunity seized for a reasonable investment of resources and within a reasonable timeline? • Answer 1: Yes, we believe that a limited amount of time investment will be required to identify, recruit, and engage three members for a board of advisors based on our network. • Question 2: Should we prioritize the solving of the problem or the seizing of the opportunity as one of our top five priorities to position the business for success and/or avoid failure? • Answer 2: Yes, as we have tried our own efforts and hired multiple sale and business development leads to increase revenue without success.	Since the answer is "yes" to both questions, the problem and opportunity card will be moved to planning.

Table 4.2. Decision-Making Stage-Gates—Governance Example

Our example has a result that is a prioritized problem or opportunity. Therefore, according to our methodology, we should proceed to planning by creating an initiative planning charter—designating a leader, assembling the right team, determining key steps for future implementation, identifying the right resources, developing the right communications strategies, and determining the estimated timelines for implementation. As noted in our methodology, we will need to consider how to ensure that this proposed change to create a better foundation for our business will be positive for the company and perceived as positive by our team members and stakeholders. Similarly, we need to ensure that implementation timeline estimates are reasonable in the context of other activities but also are aggressive, so we do not squander our most precious resource—time.

An example of this planning process in action through an illustrative initiative planning charter is shown in Table 4.3.

INITIATIVE PLANNING CHARTER—GOVERNANCE EXAMPLE

Initiative Title	Board of Advisors
Problem/Opportunity and Initiative Summary	Develop a board of advisors—initially of no more than three members—to support governance. Each individual should have an understanding of our business industry and potential sales contacts. Some modest consulting payments and a small amount of stock options will be provided as compensation to align interests between the advisors and our company.
Planning Leader	Gabrielle Turner
Planning Team Members	Gabrielle Turner Javier Soto Grace Chang

Key Implementation Steps	• Confirm board of advisors charter, participant briefing, compensation model, meeting agenda, meeting schedule, and legal agreements • Develop list of potential candidates • Prioritize potential candidates • Recruit and secure potential candidates based on prioritization
Resources Needed	• Executive team time needed for (1) charter and briefing development and (2) candidate identification, prioritization, and recruitment • Human resources time needed for board of advisor member onboarding
Communications Strategy and Steps	• Develop talking points for management team and entire team to discuss role of board of advisors; discuss first in management team meeting and then all-hands meeting • Develop talking points about board of advisors members; discuss first in management team meeting and then all-hands meeting
Key Implementation Timelines	• + ~30 days—Draft of charter, briefing, compensation model, meeting agenda, meeting schedule, and legal agreements • + ~7 days—Final charter, briefing, compensation model, meeting agenda, meeting schedule, and legal agreements/discussion of plan and team • + ~7 days—List of potential candidates • + ~10 days—Prioritization of candidates • + ~21 days—Finalization of recruitment • + ~15 days—Announcement to entire team • + ~15 days—Launch with first board of advisors meeting

Table 4.3. Initiative Planning Charter—Governance Example

With planning complete (and hopefully approved for implementation), we then move to the most critical step in the process—implementation. This step can rely on our initiative planning charter tool as the key input. We designate a leader for implementation, empower the utilization of the right team members and resources, establish an implementation monitoring protocol, develop a schedule for the key implementation steps, establish a mechanism for identifying and managing unforeseen issues and obstacles, and determine the required final activity for initial implementation completion. As with the planning activities, we will need to consider how to ensure this initiative will be positive for the business and perceived as positive by our team members and stakeholders. Similarly, we need to ensure the implementation charter is updated as issues and obstacles occur, including adjusting dates for execution, while keeping reasonably aggressive timelines.

An example of this planning process in action through an illustrative initiative implementation charter is shown in Table 4.4.

INITIATIVE IMPLEMENTATION CHARTER–GOVERNANCE EXAMPLE

Initiative Title	Board of Advisors
Problem/Opportunity and Initiative Summary	Develop a board of advisors—initially of no more than three members—to support governance. Each individual should have an understanding of our business industry and have potential sales contacts. Some modest consulting payments and a small amount of stock options will be provided as compensation to align interests between the advisors and our company.
Implementation Leader	Gabrielle Turner
Implementation Team Members	Gabrielle Turner Javier Soto Grace Chang

Implementation Resources	• Executive team time needed for (1) charter and briefing development and (2) candidate identification, prioritization, and recruitment • Human resources time needed for board of advisor member onboarding
Implementation Monitoring Protocol	Weekly status updates during weekly management team meeting
Key Implementation Steps and Schedule	• June 1—Kickoff and discussion with management team • June 15—Draft of charter, briefing, compensation model, meeting agenda, meeting schedule, and legal agreements • June 22—Final charter, briefing, compensation model, meeting agenda, meeting schedule, and legal agreements/discussion of plan with team • June 30—List of potential candidates • July 10—Prioritization of candidates • July 31—Finalization of recruitment • August 15—Announcement to entire team • August 31—Launch with first board of advisors meeting • September 7—Assessment of first meeting by implementation team
Issues/Obstacles Encountered and Resulting Implementation Plan Changes	None encountered to date (and no changes to plan)
Final Activity Required for Initial Implementation Completion	Assessment of first meeting by implementation team

Table 4.4. Initiative Implementation Charter—Governance Example

In this chapter, we examined governance models and governance team composition as one of the eight critical and strategic decision categories for small- and medium-sized businesses. I hope you found the content to be useful as you determine how to proceed with governance activities for your business. With this streamlined methodology and tools, you can transform your governance team (one of the eight critical and strategic decision categories) to position your business ventures for future successes—provided you want to do the work to get there.

IN REVIEW

What did we learn from this chapter?

1. Governance provides a structure and processes to help manage and guide a business—integrated with the activities of the management team—to help set the direction of the company, monitor the execution of these strategies, and revisit the direction. As a result, governance—in the form of a security council—should be important to you, because it impacts you, your business partners, your family, your team members, your customers, and your other stakeholders.

2. There are many options for a governance structure that are not mutually exclusive and vary in formality and authority, including the following:

    a. Board of directors—Formal group of legally defined elected individuals with the power to set business policies for management and oversight

    b. Advisory board—Informal body of experts and advisors that is generally not legally defined, constituted, or empowered, but rather is selected, constituted, and operated by the executives and management team to provide strategic advice without management or oversight authority

c. Professional advisor team—Group of professionals with specific expertise who serve as strategic advisors to executive management and/or a board without any specific legal authority; the group may or may not have a formalized structure

d. Friends and family council—Group of friends and family members responsible for providing strategic advice without any specific legal authority; the group may or may not have a formalized structure

e. Hero ball—The power of one or two self-appointed "decider" or "deciders"

3. To make the right governance choices for you and your business, you need to consider governance structure options, operational models, and governance team composition to meet your specific business needs.

To help get ready for the work you will do to improve your governance structures and team after reading this book, it is worth answering the following four questions. These opportunities for reflection will help you determine how to properly build the future governance model for your business.

FOR FURTHER EXPLORATION

What type of business governance structure do you utilize today and who is involved?

_____

_____

_____

_____

What problems are created and what opportunities are missed based on your current governance model and team?

_____

_____

_____

_____

How could you improve your business governance structure?

_____

_____

_____

_____

What governance team member backgrounds and roles are you lacking? Who might be good candidates for governance team members to fill these roles?

_____

_____

_____

_____

5

YOUR TEAM EVERY DAY

"Great things in business are never done by one person;
they're done by a team of people."

—STEVE JOBS

Now that we have covered the approaches, methodologies, and tools you can use to rethink your governance model and governance team, we can turn our efforts to the team that will provide complementary strategic guidance and daily tactical support.

How do you feel about your management team members? Do they provide you with the directional and implementation support that you need for your business to be a success? Do they do so in a complementary manner to your governance model? And are your management team members aligned to the needs of you and your business?

Or do the members of your management team and their intra-team dynamics contribute to your stress rather than help you sleep easier and get more done? Do the tensions within your team sometimes lead to a turbulent environment that puts a drag on movement toward positive results?

As important as your governance team is to the trajectory of your business, the people who help you guide and execute your business activities on a day-to-day basis are equally, or perhaps more, important. After all, as many have said before in countless ways—it is not difficult to generate visions, but making those visions happen is incredibly difficult.

In the same way that it is critical to avoid falling prey to hero ball for governance matters that provide the structure and process to help manage and guide a business, it is equally crucial to avoid these same tendencies to go it alone on the operational management of your business.

You may recall from Chapter 1 that our expert business leaders revisited their business model, plan, and strategy with their management team more regularly with their management team than with their governance team or business partners (albeit by a narrow count). More telling, perhaps, is the information from Chapter 3. These business leaders indicated that "not building the right management team" was a business misstep that more than 60 percent of them had made. This response was picked by the highest number of business leaders and outpaced picking the wrong business partners, selecting the wrong business model, and all other options.

If we know that management teams are important, and maybe even the most important element of the eight critical and strategic decision categories (at least based on the experiences of our business leader experts), how should you go about examining the right way to build or rebuild the management team for your business? Fortunately, our approaches, methodologies, and tools can be utilized to help you optimize your management team. Before diving into how to apply the components of the framework, we will examine the context for your management team decisions. We will explore four aspects of your management team: management team models to support growth, management team composition, management team operations, and management team compensation to align activities with business goals.

Management Team Models and Composition

When you consider the models and composition of management teams, there is no perfect formula for the structure, size, and combinations of talent. There are, however, three key themes that have helped small- to medium-sized business founders, owners, and leaders to build and rebuild strong management teams that help achieve business successes. These key themes are:

1. Balancing size and functional alignment

2. Examining your strengths and the strengths of your existing team

3. Seeking diversity of experiences and views

Balancing Size and Functional Alignment

You might have a few key questions: How many of our team members should I consider as part of my management team? How many team members would be too many? How many would be too few?

The answers are complex—and like many of the decisions you will make about your business, there is not a "one size fits all" solution. The right number for your business should be based on the three key themes—your team's capabilities and responsibilities, the balancing of functions and numbers, and seeking diversity of views.

But perhaps you want something more concrete. While the answer is for you to decide, I can give you some parameters based on my experience guiding and advising small- and medium-sized businesses. At the scale of business with which we are operating, it should be more than two people and likely less than ten individuals, which is still a small enough group to allow for productive conversations and representation from all parts of your business.

Why? Many of us have forged business ventures with other partners. Each of us likely can testify that the easiest way to make sure you avoid making the necessary changes and adjustments to your business is to have the decision rest in the hands of two individuals.

Does that mean that three is the right number when it comes to management teams? Perhaps it is—in some instances, with the smallest businesses. But three is definitely a minimum for a management team.

"The power of three," "the rule of three," or "three is the magic number." These phrases have been used since ancient times to describe the fascinating and compelling strength of this number. Many have recited the great love that Greek philosopher Pythagoras had for the number three—it was a "perfect" number symbolizing, among other things, the beginning, middle, and end[11] (which all things tend to have). Closer to our own times, one of my favorite songs from the days of driving my children to induce long overdue naps was "The Three R's" by Jack Johnson, in which he sings that "three, it's a magic number." Turning back to the business world, many articles, including some by leading business publisher *Inc.*, have been written about Apple's "obsession with the magical number three."[12]

In reality, three is not always the right number for a management team, but it is the smallest "right" number based on more than twenty years of business experience. Three, after all, has the "magical" quality of generally not allowing for "tied" votes on the critical and strategic decisions that will help position your business for success.

While it may or may not be three, the best number for you really depends on the scale of your business and your functional management alignment. The most important premise for the management team size— based on my experience and observations—is to make sure the size of your management team facilitates having good dialogues and making sound decisions. If you have a management team that is too large, it will often mean that much-needed debates on strategy or operations do not occur—or worse, that decisions are not made. When your management

---

11   Christiane L. Joost-Gaugier, *Measuring Heaven: Pythagoras and His Influence on Thought and Art in Antiquity and the Middle Ages* (Ithaca, New York: Cornell University Press, 2006).

12   Carmine Gallo, "Apple Is Obsessed with the Magical Number 3. It Will Transform Your Presentations, Too," *Inc.*, July 15, 2020, https://www.inc.com/carmine-gallo/apple-is-obsessed-with-magical-number-3-it-will-transform-your-presentations-too.html.

team feels like they are enduring a series of lectures, rather than partici-pating in round-table discussions, they may feel disenfranchised and start looking for the exits. You and your business will suffer as a result.

So, the number is produced through a little art and a little science once you have set the floor at three and the ceiling at nine. What do you factor into this alchemy?

Examining Your Strengths and Those of Your Existing Team

You need to make sure that all of your core business functions are rep-resented on the management team. A management team that does not represent all facets of the business will—without question—lead to feelings of disenfranchisement among your team. This means your man-agement model and your management team composition need to align to your business organizational structures and management reporting lines. When you are building and rebuilding your management teams, it is important to ensure there is a clear process for the flow of information, concerns, and recommendations from every part of the business to the management team.

Two points on the alignment of business functions merit empha-sis and some associated words of caution. First, the management team members who represent the organizational functions need to have man-agerial authority and organizational accountability for those functions. If not, comments like "The HR team is not really represented in the management team meetings" will occur and, in this scenario, the stew-ards of your talent will leave. Second, you need to be careful not to overload your hardest-working team members with too many respon-sibilities and too many voices to represent. Candidly, I am guilty of this habit—both regarding taking on the management of too many organi-zational functions and loading up my best-performing team members with too many responsibilities.

Occasionally, I refer to both myself and some of my favorite work col-leagues as a "Professional Swiss Army Knife." If you have used this type of multi-tool that unites various blades and other tools such as screw-drivers, a can opener, a corkscrew, a bottle opener, and a pair of scissors around a pivot point pin, you might get what I mean. To me, it is the best way to describe someone who can represent multiple business functions. For instance, someone like me—technology inventor by temperament, attorney by training, designer by interest, and financial modeler by necessity—would fall under this description. Other strong utility players may be adept at some other combination of skills, such as product marketing, sales, and talent recruiting.

In small- to medium-sized businesses, these are the teammates that we load up with responsibilities and reporting functions. In management structures, it can lead to odd clusters of representative constituencies—often with tensions. I have witnessed organizations that find talented compliance players who are leading compliance functions. The organizations then ask them to add responsibilities in logical areas like audit and risk management. That type of functional expansion works. But in other circumstances, the same utility players are asked to take on other growth-oriented leadership roles such as strategic planning and new initiative management. Those expansions of roles tend to fail. The same problem occurs many times with talented sales leaders who end up with too many operational and administrative responsibilities, which negatively impact their happiness and the business's top-line growth.

When you load up your hardworking talent with too many functional responsibilities, they ultimately will get burned out, whether mentally or physically. This will have the undesirable outcome of undermining the well-being of your team members and your business. You need to make sure that all functional areas of the business are represented on your management team while resisting the temptation to overload your most talented team members. Also, since you have probably already overloaded yourself, try to shift some of your responsibilities to other management team members.

Seeking Diversity of Experience and Views

When considering the backgrounds and roles you need from your management team members, it is helpful to take an approach similar to the one we used when creating our governance team. Your management team needs are often driven by your needs for additional expertise and perspectives to complement your own capabilities and biases and those of your business partners. As a result, to determine the profile of your management team, one of the best activities you can perform is to look at the eight critical and strategic decision areas and the additional context areas to assess where you need additional support.

When we are looking at aligning management team responsibilities and recruiting new talent to fill those roles (and maybe unburden some of our team members who have too many areas of responsibility), there is another tendency we need to avoid: the tendency to be attracted to people who look like us, think like us, and sound like us. This should not be terribly surprising since multiple psychological studies have indicated that humans tend to be drawn toward the familiar, especially when seeking out other people.[13]

We have all seen the trends that happen. Great sales-oriented CEOs often select other "revenuers" (as you may have heard them called). As a result, they end up with a culture that is built on growth but not in balance with compliance, which can produce significant legal and regulatory consequences. Or compliance-oriented CEOs who over-invest in operations and administrative functions but cannot make a decision that supports sales growth and increases in profitability. What we really need is balance in the composition of the management team in terms of experiences and views.

As you know, and as many wise souls have previously noted, when you stay in a bubble, surrounding yourself with like-minded people, you keep your world very small and the ideas that enter your world very limited. It is important to be open to discourse and work with people with whom

---

13   Jamie Ducharme, "Why Do So Many Couples Look Alike? Here's the Psychology Behind the Weird Phenomenon," *Time*, April 4, 2019, https://time.com/5553817/couples-who-look-alike/.

you have nothing in common. These new perspectives that open a new world could be the difference between staying on a course that is destined to fail or finding a new path that could result in success.

You do not necessarily need to administer Myers-Briggs personality tests or consider complex options for measuring cognitive diversity, but you should consider your own strengths and the strengths of your team. You should also consider how you and your business would benefit from adding people with different experiences and views when you are adding talent or restructuring your management team.

As you evaluate your existing team's capabilities, you can build strength by engaging new perspectives and mindsets when you are building and rebuilding your management team. For me, this not only means considering diversity, equity, and inclusion (DE&I), but also remembering that the two areas where I tend to need help are sales and detailed operational management practices. As noted earlier, I am not a natural salesperson. I tend to gravitate to ideas rather than tracking, so I need support on the detailed work that it takes to execute the plans. That is why I look for DE&I opportunities that support the personal sales and operational management weaknesses I need to offset. Similarly, a little analysis of your strengths and those of your team will lead you to the diversity of experiences and views that are right for you and your business.

Management Team Operations

Having reviewed concepts that are significant considerations for your management team model and composition, it is important to consider the operational model for your management team—just as it was for your governance team. Operations of this team can logically be divided into two components: content and processes.

Content for Your Management Team

When you examine content for the management team, what topics should you consider during your activities?

As you might guess, based on our research, the eight critical and strategic business decision categories should play an extraordinarily strong role:

- Governance structure and team

- Management team and compensation

- Adjustments and pivots

- Growth and infrastructure development

- Business disputes and breakups

- Acquisitions, mergers, exits, and other business transactions

- Disaster preparedness

- Succession planning

As with the governance team, it is also important to ensure that your management team has the right context and information to advise you and help you make these critical and strategic decisions. For instance, you may want to provide them with the following:

- Financial reports

- Sales and marketing updates

- Market trend information

- Technology trend information

- Corporate best practices of peers or aspirational companies

- Legal, regulatory, and compliance issues

As with the governance team, there is no perfect model for covering these topics in terms of how to visit, how often to address, and how to determine when actions are required based on the topics.

What is important is that your management team processes start from a point of alignment around the mission of the business and its future and that your structure does not induce boredom, frustration, and a feeling of a theater performance rather than outcomes.

Management Team Processes—Meetings and Beyond

Unfortunately, in nearly two decades of working with small- and medium-sized businesses, I have found that many management team members are dissatisfied with the operations of the teams in terms of meetings and the other ways that they stay engaged with one another and senior leadership.

The most common mistake I have seen from management teams, even in high-growth organizations, is that the management team operations—including how meetings happen, what the meetings involve, and how the meetings are conducted—do more harm than good. When management team members feel like their involvement in meetings equates, for instance, to participation in a "show-and-tell" session for senior executives rather than purpose-driven engagements in which they are treated as valued stakeholders with important insights and opinions, it leads to trouble for you and your business. Unfortunately, negative comments tend to happen when the management team operations are not well coordinated, collaborative, or are operated by outside parties on a regular basis.

What is the best model for operations? Unlike the governance team operations, there is often no formal legal requirement in the bylaws or operating agreements for management team operations. While that is not always the case, you often have more latitude for decisions about management team operations than governance team operations.

To put it simply, the best practices consist of a regular schedule of meetings with collaborative development of agendas that focus on the most important priorities for your management team including the following:

1. Learning through contextual and meaningful education

2. Reviewing monthly performance results

3. Discussing needs for potential adjustments

4. Deciding about next steps and future activities

As a side note, the most common time that I recommend utilizing outside consultants or other subject matter experts for management team activities is to support the learning process. The delivery of practical knowledge and wisdom is a viable role for people who can bring new and outside perspectives. Engaging outside consultants in management team reviews, discussions, and decisions more often than not will create the negative consequence of making your management team feel disrespected and undervalued.

If you feel that there is not much to learn, review, discuss, or decide (at any moment in time), do not force the meeting to occur. Time is too valuable to meet without a compelling reason.

But when you do meet, make sure that some things are clearly understood and executed. Everyone on your management team should have input on the meeting agendas. Everyone on your management team should be encouraged to speak and to bring ideas from the members of their functional teams to a safe environment for sharing and discussion. Action items and decisions should be chronicled and confirmed, in writing, to make sure the items on the agenda are addressed after the meeting.

In addition, you should make sure your team is clear on what is and is not appropriate in terms of communications from the management team meetings to the broader team at your business. Any confusion will mean unequal access to information and ultimately lead to troubles with team dynamics and business culture.

In addition to the regular meetings, one-on-one meetings should be convened on a regular basis with each functional leader and the top executive (or executives) to assess alignment of the meetings and the needs of management leaders. When you have a sense that internal conflict is brewing between management team leaders or functional teams, you should have special intervention meetings to address the issues—quickly. If the issues go beyond personalities, they should be on the agenda for the next management team meeting.

Since meetings are only one of the ways that management teams should stay engaged with one another, as with the governance team, you likely will want to develop a plan to transmit information in a way that allows your management team to help your business succeed. But it should not lead to information overload that minimizes their ability to perform their day-to-day functions. With technology constantly evolving and the workplace communications needs of teams differing from one team to another, it is important to decide as a group the best way to communicate between meetings and to support meetings and actions that flow from decisions that come from the management meetings. As with the governance team meeting model, your management team operations—outside of meetings—should also be driven by the will of your management team. In short, you need to play the way they want to play—or pick a different group of teammates.

Management Team Compensation

As a final topic on management teams, it is important to align the compensation of your management team to the objectives that you and your business owners have for your business. Only you will know the compensation that your business can tolerate for your management team and your other team members. Compensation might include cash, fringe benefits, ownership stakes, and profit participation.

Compensation Complaints

We likely have all heard complaints about how "unfair" the differing compensation models for dissimilar roles may be within a company. But, in reality, most organizations have a built-in bias to pay "producers"—the management team members and other teammates who either drive revenue growth through sales activities or provide strong profitability through service delivery.

Frankly, most of us who lead small- and medium-sized businesses tend to fit one—or more likely both—of these descriptions. Since we probably all want to be compensated reasonably well for the demanding work, sleepless nights, and stress we endure, we tend to compensate others who also produce quite well. Unfortunately, this means we occasionally tend to ignore the compensation that our operations teammates—even our best performers—might merit. I am not recommending that your legal and compliance team lead be compensated the same as your sales leader. Only you know whether that makes sense. What I do advocate is to align their mindsets and their compensation elements.

For example, I grew up playing soccer in the United States (or football or fútbol, as the rest of the world calls it). In the "beautiful game," nearly every player on the field—or pitch—has a responsibility to play offensive and defensive roles. Unfortunately, this tactical model is not in place at very many businesses, and the dynamics of your team and your business suffer as a result.

One business I advised had—by their own admission—an aggressive sales culture driven by a team that saw revenue growth as paramount. Unfortunately, the compensation model for the sales management team and sales personnel was aligned to top-line growth but not to profitability or compliance. Senior executives were also compensated based on top-line growth and profitability. Operational leaders, including legal, compliance, human resources, and other similar areas had incentives that aligned with regulatory compliance and profitability. Do you see the tension? It is not hard to spot. In soccer/football/fútbol terms, when the forward line of your team focuses only on scoring and your defenders focus only on not giving up goals, your team is not likely to be successful. And your box-to-box midfielders are likely to suffer from extreme exhaustion trying to make up for the lack of connection among their teammates. The same issues were at play in this business; sales leaders were trying to score, while the operational team was trying to avoid yielding scores.

Compensation Aligned Holistically to Objectives

A better approach is to align management compensation and compensation for your entire team to similar goals that map to the reality of your circumstances in a holistic matter. This might mean uniting revenue growth (or sustainment in tough times), profitability, and compliance (especially in heavily regulated businesses). And it might mean balancing near-term and long-term targets to avoid overheating the business. Just as importantly, be clear about this approach in writing and in conversations and explain what goals will trigger the incentive compensation for your management team and others.

Now that we have reviewed management team models and composition, operations, and compensation, we will look at how to operate our process of assessing, deciding, planning, and implementing critical and strategic decisions about our management team. We will apply our blueprint to an example.

Applying the Blueprint

Let us look at how we can apply our methodologies and tools to examine this second critical and strategic decision question set: How can I build the right management team, and what is the best way to engage and compensate my team members to meet my business goals?

As with the governance question, we will use a fictional example that is a composite of a number of companies I have been involved with. This example will illustrate the application of the methodologies and tools from our blueprint to this management team question. It is important to bear in mind that you likely will generate more than one card when you advance your process, and the concepts that we use in this chapter are just one example to support your own activities.

We will start our management team assessment phase by exploring the problems or opportunities that exist for our business and its management team. This involves an assessment of the management team model, composition, topical knowledge, capabilities (and gaps), operations, and compensation structures that currently propel the activities of the business.

Then, for each problem or opportunity, we ask the detailed questions related to background and context, impact on future success or failure, constraints with solving the problem or meeting the opportunity, expected benefits to solving the problem or meeting the opportunity, and options for solving the problem or meeting the opportunity. An example of this assessment phase for exploring potential management team improvements to support business success based on our fictional company is shown in Table 5.1.

PROBLEM AND OPPORTUNITY CARD—MANAGEMENT EXAMPLE

Problem/Opportunity Title	Management Team Meetings
Problem/Opportunity Summary	Our management team meetings have become stale, and our team complains that the time together is wasted. There has to be a better way to use our time together.
Background/Context	Our management team meetings have vacillated between two forms—unorganized, free-flowing, round-robin discussions or facilitated exercises led by outside consultants.
Impact and Alignment to Future Success or Failure	Management team being directed toward outcomes that would support business goals and objectives, as well as serve to motivate the management team.
Constraints on Solving/ Meeting	We cannot afford to spend more than one to two hours per week in management team meetings.
Benefits of Solving/ Meeting	Better meetings will make for better business performance.
Options for Solving/ Meeting	We could restructure the meetings to sequentially—each month—focus on the following: learning, reviewing performance, discussing needs and adjustments, and making decisions.
Applicable Category	Management
Prioritization	High—subject to decision-making process
Status	Awaiting decision-making about prioritization

Table 5.1. Problem and Opportunity Card—Management Example

After the assessment phase, we move from analysis and conceptualization to decision-making about management team changes in terms of models, composition, operations, and compensation.

Following our method, we recommend the same two-step stage-gates process to identify initiatives for further evaluation and prioritization, parking lot items, and archived concepts. Using our standard criteria, we take our problem and opportunity card example from Table 5.1 and apply the objective criteria to guide selection of the priorities for planning and implementation, as in the example in Table 5.2.

In our example, we determined that this is a prioritized problem or opportunity. Therefore, under our methodology, we proceed to the planning stage and create an initiative planning charter with the key details that set the stage for potential implementation: planning leader and team, key steps and resources for future implementation, communications strategies, and estimated timelines for implementation. According to our methodology, we will need to consider how to ensure this proposed change creates a better foundation for our business, our team, and our stakeholders. Similarly, we need to ensure that the implementation timeline estimates are reasonable but aggressive in the context of other activities.

An example of this planning process in action through an initiative planning charter follows in Table 5.3.

With planning complete (and hopefully approved for implementation), we move to the most critical step in the process—implementation. During this phase, we will rely on our initiative planning charter tool as a stepping stone. As with the governance team, we focus on delineating the key implementation items: the leader and team, resources, schedule, monitoring protocol, mechanism for identifying and managing unforeseen issues and obstacles, and the required final activity for initial completion. As with the planning activities, we will need to consider how to ensure this initiative will be positive for the company, our team members, and stakeholders. Similarly, we need to ensure the implementation charter is updated as issues and obstacles occur, including adjusting dates for execution, while keeping reasonable timelines.

DECISION-MAKING STAGE-GATES—MANAGEMENT EXAMPLE

Problem/ Opportunity Title	Management Team Meetings	
Stage-Gate #	**Questions to Answer**	**Result**
Stage-Gate 1	• Question 1: Does the problem or opportunity cause a loss of revenue, loss of profit margin, loss of employees, misalignment of our mission, or other potential failure? • Answer 1: Yes. Our management team's operational problems may lead to a loss of team members and other business problems. • Question 2: Does the solution represent an opportunity to increase revenue, margins, team stability, business alignment to mission, or future success? • Answer 2: Yes. A new management team operations approach could help stabilize the management team and also align our activities better for future success. • Question 3: Does the problem or opportunity merit potential prioritization despite not eliciting a "yes" to one of the preceding questions? • Answer 3: Non-applicable, as the answers to both Question 1 and Question 2 are "yes."	Since the answer is "yes" to the first two questions, the problem and opportunity card will be moved to decision-making stage-gate 2.
Stage-Gate 2	• Question 1: Can the problem be solved or opportunity seized for a reasonable investment of resources and within a reasonable timeline? • Answer 1: Yes, we believe that a new management team meeting construct that sequentially focuses on learning, reviewing performance, discussing needs and adjustments, and making decisions could help us to solve the problem with little time and work effort. • Question 2: Should we prioritize the solving of the problem or the seizing of the opportunity as one of our top five priorities to position the business for success and/or avoid failure? • Answer 2: Yes, because we risk losing management team interest and alignment if we do not make a change in management team operations.	Since the answer is "yes" to both questions, the problem and opportunity card will be moved to planning.

Table 5.2. Decision-Making Stage-Gates—Management Example

INITIATIVE PLANNING CHARTER—MANAGEMENT EXAMPLE

Initiative Title	Management Team Meeting Operations Update
Problem/ Opportunity and Initiative Summary	Develop a management team meeting operational construct to focus, sequentially, each month, on the following: learning through contextual and meaningful education, reviewing business performance, discussing emerging business needs and adjustments, and making decisions
Planning Leader	Camila Martinez
Planning Team Members	Camila Martinez Javier Soto Gabrielle Turner Sean Williams
Key Implementation Steps	• Confirm meeting agendas, learning plan, and other content • Develop list of learning plan topics and presenters • Finalize business performance review items • Determine discussion and decision-making approaches
Resources Needed	• Executive team time needed for agenda development, learning plan, and discussion/decision models • Executive and human resources time needed for learning plan coordination
Communications Strategy and Steps	Develop talking points for management team to discuss new management team operational construct and to solicit input on learning plan
Key Implementation Timelines	• + ~15 days—Draft of agendas, learning plan, and discussion/ decision models • + ~7 days—Final agendas, learning plan (and initial presenter), and models • + ~7 days—Launch of new management team meeting construct • + ~15 days—Draft list of next five presenters for learning plan

Table 5.3. Initiative Planning Charter—Management Example

INITIATIVE IMPLEMENTATION CHARTER—MANAGEMENT EXAMPLE

Initiative Title	Management Team Meeting Operations Update
Problem/Opportunity and Initiative Summary	Develop a management team meeting operational construct to focus, sequentially, each month, on the following: learning through contextual and meaningful education, reviewing business performance, discussing emerging business needs and adjustments, and making decisions
Implementation Leader	Camila Martinez
Implementation Team Members	Ali Kamgar Gabrielle Turner Camila Martinez Javier Soto Grace Chang Sean Williams
Implementation Resources	• Executive team time needed for agenda development, learning plan, and discussion/decision models • Executive and human resources time needed for learning plan coordination
Implementation Monitoring Protocol	Weekly status updates during weekly management team meeting
Key Implementation Steps and Schedule	• October 1—Kickoff and discussion with management team • October 16—Draft of agendas, learning plan (and initial presenter), and models • October 31—Final agendas, learning plan (and initial presenter), and models • November 1—Launch of new management team meeting construct • November 15—Draft list of next five presenters for learning plan • December 1—Assessment of first meeting by implementation team
Issues/Obstacles Encountered and Resulting Implementation Plan Changes	None encountered to date (and no changes to plan)
Final Activity Required for Initial Implementation Completion	Assessment of each of the meetings during the first month of the implementation by the full management team

Table 5.4. Initiative Implementation Charter—Management Example

An example of this planning process in action through an illustrative initiative implementation charter is shown in Table 5.4, on the preceding page.

In this chapter, we explored management team models, composition, engagement, and compensation as one of the eight critical and strategic decision categories for small- and medium-sized businesses. I hope the content emboldens you to examine potential opportunities to update and improve your management structures and processes. By applying this streamlined methodology and our tools, you can transform your management team and position your business ventures for future successes.

IN REVIEW

What did we learn from this chapter?

1. To make the right management team choices for you and your business, you need to consider management team models and composition, operational structures, and compensation approaches to meet your specific business needs.

2. Three key themes have helped small- to medium-sized business founders, owners, and leaders build and rebuild strong management teams that help achieve business success:

   a. Balancing management team size and functional alignment

   b. Examining the strengths that you and your existing management team possess

   c. Seeking diversity of experiences and views for your management team

3. Management teams will benefit from a regularized schedule of meetings with collaborative development of agendas that focus on the most important priorities for your management team:

   a. Learning through contextual and meaningful education

   b. Reviewing monthly performance results

c. Discussing needs for and potential adjustments

d. Deciding about next steps and future activities

4. Your management team and your business performance will be optimized by aligning management compensation and compensation for your entire team to goals that map to the reality of your business circumstances in a holistic matter—uniting revenue targets, profitability, and compliance while balancing near-term and long-term targets.

To help get ready for the work you will do to update your management team models and structures after reading this book, consider the following four questions. These questions will help you determine how to properly build the future management organizational approaches you need for your business.

FOR FURTHER EXPLORATION

What is the structure and composition of your management team today, and what are its strengths and weaknesses?

_____

_____

_____

_____

What problems are created and what opportunities have you missed based on your current management team and its weaknesses?

_____

_____

_____

_____

How could you improve your business-management structure and compensation models?

_____

_____

_____

_____

What could you do to improve your business-management team (and who might be involved)?

_____

_____

_____

_____

6

ADJUSTMENTS
AND PIVOTS

"Pivoting isn't Plan B: It's part of the process."

—JEFF GOINS

Sometimes your business model and business strategy might need to be reinvented entirely or, at a minimum, modified in some way. If you have led a business, you likely have experienced the feeling that something was not quite right with the trajectory of your business—or you might even have empirical data from your financial reports and sales pipelines.

How did you approach that gut instinct or striking information? Did you initially ignore—or worse, fully ignore—the signals? How did that play out? Did delaying an analysis of what needed to change end up compromising the potential for your business to succeed? Or did you work quickly from a perspective that your business plan and strategy (which had either served you well or helped you to launch) might need a refresh—and, as a result, did you achieve success?

In Chapter 1, we examined the additional context that powers the approaches, methodologies, and tools that help create a strong foundation—time after time—when applied to the eight critical and strategic decision categories that are most important for driving your business success. We looked at two of the areas of the additional contexts that should be combined with your own firsthand experiences: "Worrying Productively" and "Embracing Change." Both of these themes are critically important for you when you consider opportunities to adjust, pivot, or make critical and strategic decisions to position your business for future successes. Often, being open to these two types of thinking is what allows you to build your business better than it is today.

Worrying is second nature to me, and constructive worrying—making the worrying productive—is a skill that I developed over time. Being open to examining the signals that are facing your business today and that your business will face in the future are vital to creating the right plan for success. Further, being open to change—both architecting and implementing change—via the adjustments and pivots that need to be made to your business strategy is imperative, too. Sometimes this means making small changes that are simply adjustments, and sometimes it means being open to really significant changes—like pivots.

The first business venture that I launched with partners is a textbook example of the need to constantly assess whether to make adjustments and, occasionally, when and how to initiate major pivots to a business strategy.

We launched the business at the end of 2001 as a consulting company focused on the energy sector, which seemed ready for dynamic change with global interest in environmental management. We looked for opportunities to develop products to address the needs of our U.S. federal government and publicly traded energy company customers. After some market assessment and a deep study of global trends, we decided to make our first adjustment. We implemented a plan to reinvest our profits and raise a little bit of angel funding to build a software platform to help companies and governments manage their environmental liabilities and, potentially, their environmentally driven commodity assets.

As you read this, you might be thinking that this was a great idea, but it might have been twenty years too early for the marketplace—and you would be right. We, too, quickly realized that this market was not going to develop rapidly, if at all, and we decided it was time for another adjustment.

Instead of trying to sell the software we had built that leveraged our understanding of environmental management (and its associated need for sensor-driven, real-time monitoring), we looked for opportunities to expand our consulting business because we had developed strong capabilities in software design and development focused on building applications for real-time monitoring and control capabilities. We grew our consulting and software development revenue to nearly $5 million per year in a little less than five years from the founding of our company. While trying to grow that line of business, though, it became clear that scaling from our base in Morgantown, West Virginia, would be difficult due to a geographical lack of access to customers and the competitive market trends.

With these factors in mind, we did an informal assessment of our options. Two clear paths emerged. The first—which was simply plowing ahead—would witness us attempting to scale our consulting and software development business. We would be trying to compete for these types of software and service contracts in a market focused on national security that was rapidly being co-opted by very large enterprises like Northrop Grumman, Boeing, and SAIC, among others—some of which were competitors and some of which were customers.

The second involved a more dramatic change. As we did our productive worrying, we spotted an opportunity to do something vastly different. Our management team analyzed our consulting and software development business and identified an opportunity to create a software product for developing next-generation sensing and control applications. This opportunity would help our business build better software more quickly while selling this same product to our customers and competitors so they could do the same.

This second path would be both a massive change and a massive risk to our business. We had to pivot our business from what had become a pure services approach (after we abandoned the first environmental management software product) to a software-led and service support model. To make this second option work, we would need to invest all our resources in making a software platform that would support the service support work we were already doing, and we would sell this platform and our support services to our customers and competitors. We would also need to add additional outside investment funding. This meant refocusing our profits from sales to internal product development, raising additional outside venture capital funding, and taking on a larger line of credit secured by business owner guarantees.

Ultimately, we—both the management team and the governance team—decided to take the second path. Along the way, we created a product—EdgeFrontier—that fueled additional growth and became an early Internet of Things software platform. It now serves as a core element of some of global technology leader Hexagon AB's product offerings. Hexagon AB acquired our company in 2011 after a decade of efforts by a great group of team members.

The outcome for our company, our team, and our investors was—by most measures—positive. But we also received a second benefit. We learned a lot of lessons, such as identifying the need for change, exploring the opportunities and assets that exist (and the associated alignment), and leaning into the best options, all of which apply to adjusting and pivoting your business.

Identifying the Need for Change

As you may recall, in Chapter 1, we learned that nearly 70 percent of our surveyed group of business leaders affirmed that they have processes in place in their businesses to support assessing the need for, deciding on, planning, and implementing change. A first step in the process is usually having a process to identify the need for change.

Given that a large majority of this group of successful business leaders have processes in place, it should come as little surprise that more than

50 percent of these executives collaborate with their team—which could include both their governance team and management team—through a regularized and formal process for making adjustments and pivots, as evidenced in Figure 6.1. Conversely, less than 5 percent of these leaders were lone wolves—assessing and charting the course for change on their own. Just as significantly, a slightly smaller number (almost 40 percent of these leaders) focus on making adjustments or pivots with their team based on the urgency of specific situations.

These survey responses provide us with two important takeaways. First, adjustments and pivots should not be a "go it alone" activity. Rather, you should rely on the work you did in our first two critical and strategic decision areas—which focused on building and rebuilding your governance and management teams—to assist you with the work in this third decision area of adjustments and pivots. Second, you need to be alert to signals that will indicate when changes may be needed to your business strategy and plan.

How do you go about identifying the need for changes to your business and deciding on the potential adjustments and pivots that follow?

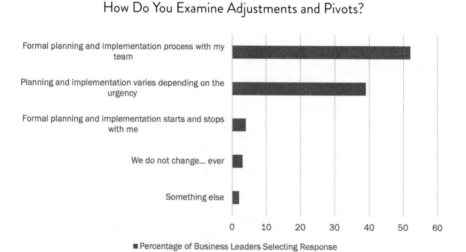

Figure 6.1

The good news is that much of what you need to do is built into your plan for creating agendas for governance teams and management teams. You can use those agendas to plan discussions about potential adjustment needs that you have identified through contextual and meaningful education and monthly reviews of the performance of the business.

Of course, it is entirely possible to sleepwalk through these activities without having your "sensors on" to listen for the cues that change is coming or should be coming at your business. You likely have been in regular monthly or weekly meetings where it feels like nearly everyone in the room is simply physically present. Their eyes are glazed over, or they are almost asleep. They are not mentally or emotionally dialed in and engaged with the discussion.

How do you and your company make your meetings and your time outside of these meetings as productive as possible to help you tune in to the signals of change?

You likely will know what is best for your business in terms of the information and data that might indicate an adjustment or pivot is needed. But there are some key items nearly all businesses should target; these include performance, education, and assessment.

Performance

Performance measurements worth reviewing (as you probably already do) with both your management and governance teams likely include results and projections for both financials and sales. Most business leadership teams that I have helped lead or advise tend to review current and projected financial performance by looking at short-term and long-term cash flows and comparative financial performance, including month-to-month and year-to-year comparisons. When examining sales results and projections, most successful teams tend to look at comparative sales results and trends. Analyzing data on deviations, trends, and their causes with your teams will help you reflect on the issues your business may face in the future, and you may be able to identify signals that indicate the need for adjustments and pivots.

In addition, most teams generally review their sales pipelines. Realistic (not overly optimistic) projections must be used to populate the sales pipeline (and the associated financial projections that rely on these forecasts). Viable projections and realistic pipelines provide the opportunity to spot when changes need to be made. Too many promising businesses—and their leaders—have been derailed by projections and pipelines that are presented through rose-colored glasses. When you do not use realistic projections and pipelines, you are not operating from a realistic view of your business. This increases the possibility that you will not make the right adjustments and pivots.

Education

In addition to having and using accurate performance information, you and your management and governance teams need to ensure that your contextual knowledge continues to grow. This will enable you to be attuned to the need for change in your business. Unfortunately, in my experience, management and governance teams focus less on these areas than on performance, which leaves these teams without critical data. Some of the types of information that your teams need are pretty intuitive—information about new products and service offerings that are competitive, external reports on market trends in your markets and similar segments, technology trends, best practices in your industry and adjacent or analogous segments, and legal, regulatory, and compliance issues that will be facing your business, customers, and markets.

I have found other types of intelligence to be very helpful to businesses I have helped to lead or advise—information from the front lines of the business. The data comes in the form of sales team feedback on the obstacles and impediments they experience, customer and prospective customer feedback on needs and wants, and feedback and observations from sales and delivery partners, if applicable.

While these other types of intelligence may not be the types of information you usually provide to your management and leadership teams (if you are collecting this content), this feedback from the tactical level of sales and delivery engagement will give you and your teams the earliest warning signs when changes are needed.

Assessment

After taking in the information from performance and education activities that might indicate changes are needed, your management and governance teams should engage in conversations about how that information might impact strategies and, potentially, what adjustments and pivots might be needed. In these dialogues, the teams should revisit assumptions about the future, consider alternatives to the current plans and future goals, and examine what assumptions and alternatives align with the signals from the performance and education activities.

If the intake of information does not contribute to a reassessment of the current and future plans (and potential adjustments and pivots), you and your team are sleepwalking and have forgotten to turn your sensors on. If you do not end up examining what the data points mean, you will probably miss the signals for change.

Bringing It All Together

This list of key items is not exhaustive, but it shows the type of details you should consider providing to your governance and management teams. It should also help you understand how much time you should spend learning, researching, and analyzing on your own. Many experts will tell you to read and explore, but the key is to assess the information after absorbing it to bring it all together.

What are the signals that should cause you to act and make adjustments or pivots? As you know from your experience, it is as much art as it is science. My advice to my business partners and the companies I counsel is this: You will know it when you see it, but you have to be looking for it.

Exploring Opportunities and Assets (and Alignment)

Once you have seen the signals that adjustments or pivots are required (and have mentally adjusted to the reality that your best-laid plans may not have been perfect), it is time to explore your options and identify the adjustments and pivots that can put you, your team, and your business on a pathway to more successful outcomes.

This exploration has two essential elements: (1) market opportunities and (2) the assets you have that can drive business growth and sustainability. The key to making the best decision—whether it is a simple adjustment or a big pivot—is to make sure both elements are aligned and can be reasonably met by your business.

What do we mean by assets? These assets could be proprietary technology, like software or products, or components of software or products that could be repurposed and enhanced in some manner. It could be existing knowledge or a specific current capability residing within your team that can be delivered as a service offering to customers and through your partners. Or it could be something new that could be built—such as a product or a service—with additional investment.

How you approach exploring these two elements—opportunities and assets—and their alignment is best left to you and your team. In my own work, I have found that a sequential approach to this exploration produces the most rational outcomes.

The first step in this process is for you and your teams to use your research and analysis to deeply explore the signals and information around the market opportunities and explore the feedback from your customers, prospective customers, and channel partners on their needs. After all, trying to sell something the market does not want will not help you succeed. The second step is to dig deeply into your business assets that can be leveraged, repurposed, or enhanced to meet these market opportunities. The final step is to assess how these assets might be best aligned to meet the market opportunities.

As you move through this process, you will want to consider the costs required to align your assets with the opportunities you identified. The salaries for the needed talent and other costs to create the product or service offerings—and to get these offerings to the market—may mean that adjustments might end up looking like better bets than pivots. In times of more pronounced urgency and dynamic market signals, though, the significant cost of pivots may be your only option. In addition, you will want to pressure-test potential outcomes and plans for adjustments or pivots with market validation from your team, current customers, channel partners, and potential new customers and partners. A leap of faith may work sometimes, but great analysis supported by validation tends to produce better results.

To conduct these exploration activities, it is usually best to do an inventory and alignment mapping of each of the opportunities and assets, and this should be updated on a regular basis such as annually or semiannually or when the signals demand an urgent assessment. Other businesses will do traditional assessments such as strength-weakness-opportunity-threat (SWOT) analyses. Whatever method you choose, it is important to revisit it regularly to ensure you do not miss the need to make changes or the potential to make the right change.

Leaning into the Best Adjustment and Pivot Option

We probably have all made adjustments to our business strategy and plan, but fewer of us may have made significant pivots. As noted early in this chapter, the team at my first business venture implemented adjustments, but they also made a really significant pivot.

What about the business leaders we surveyed? Have they, too, found pivots necessary to produce success in their business ventures? The answer is a resounding "yes." More than 75 percent of these leaders pivoted their business ventures at least one time, and an amazing 40 percent made dramatic changes three or more times as they guided their companies to strong results and sustained prosperity, as noted in Figure 6.2.

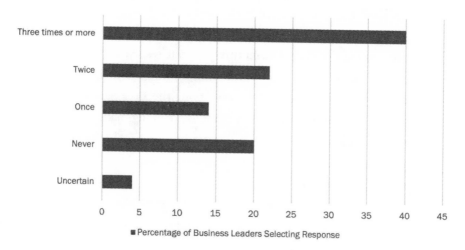

What Has Been Your Pivoting Frequency for Your Businesses?

Figure 6.2

To make adjustments or major moves like these business leaders have done—and more than 60 percent of them have done so more than once—takes commitment, the ability to embrace change, humility, and clear communication. *Inc.* columnist Scott Mautz quoted former GE CEO Jeff Immelt when writing about how difficult it is to make adjustments and pivots—even when presented with information that a business strategy (which may have worked) is not working.[14] Immelt talked about the tension between making a commitment and being open to change. He said, "Even as you're making a major commitment of resources, you've got to be open to pivoting on the basis of what you learn, because you're unlikely to get the strategy perfect out of the gate. Nothing we've done (at GE) has ever turned out exactly as it began."[15]

After you get past the need to admit there is a better path for your

---

14   Scott Mautz, "Jeff Immelt Just Nailed Why Too Many Startups Pivot Their Business Too Late," *Inc.*, October 3, 2017, https://www.inc.com/scott-mautz/jeff-immelt-just-nailed-why-too-many-startups-pivot-their-business-too-late.html.

15   Jeffrey Immelt, "How I Remade GE," *Harvard Business Review*, September–October 2017, https://hbr.org/2017/09/how-i-remade-ge.

business than the one you are currently running, your opportunity to succeed will increase—provided you and your team have done the hard work of exploring and analyzing.

Once you have made the commitment, your resolve and that of your management team need to be on full display for your entire team. You can do this by communicating clearly about the necessary directional changes that are coming, why these changes are being made to the strategy, and what the outcomes are anticipated to be for the business and every team member.

If the adjustments and pivots mean changes to the team, it will be critically important to manage those changes in the most humane way—through retraining opportunities, working severance, or other compensation packages that lead to good transitions for team members who may be negatively impacted. This is crucial not only for those who will be directly impacted, but also for your entire team.

One last point—when you lean into the adjustments or pivots, remember to keep your sensing systems in place to gather signals and information to help you perfect these plans or make more adjustments and pivots. I have found this to be necessary for each business venture I have helped lead or advise.

Applying the Blueprint

Let us explore the way we apply our methodologies and tools to examine this third critical and strategic decision question: How should I adjust or pivot my business strategy to achieve my goals?

As with the prior questions that focused on governance and management teams, we will use a fictional composite example drawn from a number of companies I have led or advised. This example will show us how to apply the methodologies and tools from our blueprint to adjust and pivot our business strategy. It is important to bear in mind that you likely will generate more than one card when you advance your process, and the concepts we use in this chapter are just one example to support your own activities.

Let us start our assessment phase for potential business strategy adjustments and pivots by exploring the problems or opportunities that exist for our business. This involves an assessment of the business strategy opportunities, our assets, and the alignment of these opportunities and assets. Then, for each problem or opportunity, we ask the detailed questions pertaining to solving or meeting the problem or opportunity with regard to background and context, impact on future success or failure, constraints, expected benefits, and options for addressing. An example of this assessment phase for exploring potential adjustment and pivot options to create the conditions for success based on our fictional company is shown in Table 6.1.

After the assessment phase, we move from analysis and conceptualization to decision-making about business strategy adjustments and pivots to assess opportunities, assets, and alignment. I recommend using the same two-step process to determine initiatives for further evaluation and prioritization—taking the problem and opportunity card example from Table 6.1 and applying the appropriate criteria to select the priorities for planning and implementation, as shown in Table 6.2.

The result in our example is a prioritized problem or opportunity; therefore, we proceed to planning by creating an initiative planning charter with a planning leader and team, key steps for future implementation, resources needed for implementation, communications strategies, and estimated timelines for implementation. We will need to consider how to ensure this proposed change to create a better foundation for our business, our team, and our stakeholders is executed. Similarly, we need to ensure implementation timeline estimates are reasonable in the context of other activities but are also aggressive to avoid squandering any opportunities or resources.

An example of this planning process in action through an illustrative initiative planning charter follows in Table 6.3.

PROBLEM AND OPPORTUNITY CARD— ADJUSTMENTS AND PIVOTS EXAMPLE

Problem/ Opportunity Title	Competitive Sales Advantage Through Software to Support Services
Problem/ Opportunity Summary	Our consulting services, which had strong differentiation when launched, are now in an increasingly crowded market.
Background/ Context	Five years ago, our company's consulting services were novel and attracted attention and customers at a strong rate—propelling growth by more than 100 percent for each of our first three years in business. Last year was not a growth year. This year, our revenues will decline by 20 percent and we will see two large engagements end. Our sales team is providing us with customer feedback that indicates there are too many other lower-cost options available that compete with our services capabilities.
Impact and Alignment to Future Success or Failure	The declining revenue and customer losses are signals that our business may be in trouble if we do not make changes to our offerings.
Constraints on Solving/Meeting	We only have $500,000 in free cash flows to reinvest to create some new differentiated capacity to help us increase sales.
Benefits of Solving/Meeting	If we generated a novel capability of some type, we may be able to keep current clients and generate new customers and revenues, as we had in the past.
Options for Solving/Meeting	We could look to launch adjacent services opportunities (but this idea does not seem to have been validated by our customers) or develop a software platform for use by our team and our clients. This platform would improve our consulting engagement, help us differentiate our business from the competition, and help increase sales and sustained client work. This simple software tool would be unique among our competition, decrease our service costs, and create stickiness with customers who use it.
Applicable Category	Business strategy adjustments
Prioritization	High—subject to decision-making process
Status	Awaiting decision-making about prioritization

Table 6.1. Problem and Opportunity Card—Adjustments and Pivots Example

DECISION-MAKING STAGE-GATES—
ADJUSTMENTS AND PIVOTS EXAMPLE

Problem/ Opportunity Title	Competitive Sales Advantages Through Software to Support Services	
Stage-Gate #	Questions to Answer	Result
Stage-Gate 1	• Question 1: Does the problem or opportunity cause a loss of revenue, loss of profit margin, loss of employees, misalignment of our mission, or other potential failure? • Answer 1: Yes. Our sales, revenue, and customer attrition problems may lead to a contraction in our business and, potentially, the demise of our business. • Question 2: Does the solution represent an opportunity to increase revenue, margins, team stability, business alignment to mission, or future success? • Answer 2: Yes. A software platform to supplement and enhance our services offerings could help stabilize our current customer engagements, position us for new sales, and drive revenue and profit growth. • Question 3: Does the problem or opportunity merit potential prioritization despite not eliciting a "yes" to one of the preceding questions? • Answer 3: Not applicable, as the answers to both Question 1 and Question 2 are "yes."	Since the answer is "yes" to the first two questions, the problem and opportunity card will be moved to decision-making stage-gate 2.
Stage-Gate 2	• Question 1: Can the problem be solved or opportunity seized for a reasonable investment of resources and within a reasonable timeline? • Answer 1: Yes, we believe that a simple software tool could help stabilize our current customer engagements, position us for new sales, and drive revenue and profit growth. • Question 2: Should we prioritize the solving of the problem or the seizing of the opportunity as one of our top five priorities to position the business for success and/or avoid failure? • Answer 2: Yes, as we risk losing more customers and sales if we do not make a change and provide a unique and differentiated capability again.	Since the answer is "yes" to both questions, the problem and opportunity card will be moved to planning.

Table 6.2. Decision-Making Stage-Gates—Adjustments and Pivots Example

INITIATIVE PLANNING CHARTER— ADJUSTMENTS AND PIVOTS EXAMPLE

Initiative Title	Software Platform for Consulting Services
Problem/Opportunity and Initiative Summary	Develop a software platform to create a value-added and differentiated tool to support our consulting services and sustained client engagement
Planning Leader	Javier Soto
Planning Team Members	Javier Soto Sofia Havel Samay Agrawal Gabrielle Turner
Key Implementation Steps	• Develop software plan document • Create initial software design concepts • Validate/update software design concepts and utility with customers and partners • Investigate commercial-off-the-shelf (COTS) options to accelerate development times and reduce costs (including outsourced development vs. internal development) • Finalize development plan and timelines
Resources Needed	• Delivery team and sales team time needed for plan, validation, and sales • Outsourced or new hires for product management, software design, and software development (estimated cost $500,000)
Communications Strategy and Steps	Develop talking points for value-proposition for internal communications and validation conversations with clients and partners
Key Implementation Timelines	• + ~30 days—Development of initial software plan • + ~20 days—Development of initial software design concepts • + ~60 days—Validations/updating of software design based on customer and partner engagement and feedback • + ~30 days—Development of software development plan • + ~180 days—Software alpha version available for use and testing

Table 6.3. Initiative Planning Charter—Adjustments and Pivots Example

INITIATIVE IMPLEMENTATION CHARTER— ADJUSTMENTS AND PIVOTS EXAMPLE

Initiative Title	Software Platform for Consulting Services
Problem/Opportunity and Initiative Summary	Develop a software platform to create a value-added and differentiated tool to support our consulting services sales and sustained client engagement
Implementation Leader	Javier Soto
Implementation Team Members	Javier Soto Sean Williams Sofia Havel Gabrielle Turner Samay Agrawal
Implementation Resources	• Delivery team and sales team time needed for planning, validation, and sales • Outsourced or new hires for product management, software design, and software development (estimated cost: $500,000)
Implementation Monitoring Protocol	• Software product planning meetings three times per week • Weekly status updates during weekly management team meeting
Key Implementation Steps and Schedule	• March 1—Kickoff and discussion with project team • April 1—Development of initial software plan • April 21—Development of initial software design concepts • June 3—Validation/updating of software design based on customer and partner engagement and feedback • July 31—Development of software development plan • January 31 (next year)—Software alpha version available for use and testing • August 1—Assessment of first six months of services plus software sales and delivery activities
Issues/Obstacles Encountered and Resulting Implementation Plan Changes	None encountered to date (and no changes to plan)
Final Activity Required for Initial Implementation Completion	Review of services plus software sales pipeline, sales outcomes, and delivery results at six months after software launch

Table 6.4. Initiative Implementation Charter—Adjustments and Pivots Example

With planning complete (and hopefully approved for implementation), we move to the most critical step in the process—implementation. We will rely on our initiative planning charter tool as a stepping stone to designate a leader and the team, verify implementation resources, establish a schedule and an implementation monitoring protocol, select a mechanism for identifying and managing unforeseen issues and obstacles, and designate the required final activity for initial completion. As with the planning activities, we need to consider how to ensure this initiative will be positive for the company, our team members, and stakeholders. Similarly, we need to update the implementation charter as issues and obstacles occur; this includes adjusting dates for execution while keeping reasonable timelines.

An example of this planning process in action through an illustrative initiative implementation charter is in Table 6.4, on the preceding page.

In this chapter, we examined options for business strategy adjustments and pivots as one of the eight critical and strategic decisions that face small- and medium-sized businesses. Ideally, you are ready to consider opportunities for potential adjustments and pivots that may help your business. By applying this streamlined methodology and tools, you can change the way you embrace and act on the need for business strategy adjustments and pivots to position your ventures for future successes.

IN REVIEW

What did we learn from this chapter?

1. To make the right business strategy adjustments and pivots for you, your team, and your business, you need to do constructive worrying and be open to embracing change.

2. Three key themes have helped small- to medium-sized business founders, owners, and leaders make the right business strategy adjustments and pivots to help achieve business successes:

a. Identifying the need for business strategy change

b. Exploring opportunities, assets, and their potential alignment

c. Leaning into adjustment and pivot options (and being open to doing it again)

3. Identifying the need for business change is something that should be occurring daily in your work (and in your governance and management team meetings) and often centers on the following:

   a. Performance (including current and projected future financial performance, comparative financial performance, and sales pipelines)

   b. Education (including sales team feedback, customer and partner survey information on needs and wants, new competitive products and service offerings, external reports on market trends, technology trends, best practices, and future relevant governmental issues)

   c. Assessment (including revisiting assumptions about the future, considering alternatives to the assumptions and plans, and examining what assumptions and alternatives align to the signals from the performance and education activities)

4. The two essential elements of exploring opportunities and assets (and the key to making the best decisions, whether it is a simple adjustment or a big pivot) is to make sure that the first element—the market opportunities—and the second—your assets that can drive business growth and sustainability—are aligned and can be reasonably met by your business.

5. When you lean into the adjustments or pivots, remember to keep your data-gathering systems in place to collect signals and information to assist you with perfecting these plans or making more adjustments and pivots.

To help get ready for examining business strategy adjustment and pivot options, please take a moment to consider the following four questions to help you determine how to properly build the structures for examining your business and making the right business strategy adjustments and pivots for your business.

FOR FURTHER EXPLORATION

How do you currently examine needs and opportunities to make adjustments to or pivots on your business strategy?

_____

_____

_____

_____

What adjustments or pivots have you missed and how could you have identified them and capitalized on them?

_____

_____

_____

_____

How will you update your business strategy adjustment and pivot planning?

_____

_____

_____

_____

What adjustment or pivot opportunities may exist today that might merit further exploration?

_____

_____

_____

_____

7

BUILDING THE ROAD
AS YOU DRIVE

"If you build castles in the air, your work
need not be lost; that is where they should be.
Now put the foundations under them."

—HENRY DAVID THOREAU

Most of us want to successfully grow and scale our business ventures. Those of us who do not seek increased revenues and larger enterprises generally want to sustain our current ventures. In either scenario, the infrastructure required to support you, your team, and your business will change as a result of growth or other factors such as evolutions in technology, business processes, operational approaches, facilities, and your team.

Many small business leaders joke about building the road as they drive the bus down it. Others talk about building castles in the sky without proper foundations. Unfortunately, our desire to grow without first building the support structures can be as dangerous as it sounds. Why do we do this to ourselves, our teams, and our businesses?

If you often (or even occasionally) fall prey to this tendency to only invest in infrastructure as you arrive at the need for it, you are certainly not alone. You may recall times—as I do from my firsthand experiences leading businesses and advising other executives on leading their companies—when you drove a little ahead of the road-building activities or failed to invest in foundation expansions. And, as a result, you ran your business off the road or watched it teeter toward collapse.

It is tricky to determine what infrastructure to build and how to build it to support growth without killing profitability or sacrificing the engines that are driving the current successes of your business. You may have made mistakes similar to the ones I have helped many business leaders address, such as launching internal infrastructure initiatives that began to distract from the work of sales and delivery to customers. These initiatives were detrimental to their businesses and frustrated the team members responsible for sales and the fulfillment of client engagements.

How do you strike the right balance on building internal infrastructure? How do you manage the need to develop your business infrastructure to support growth without strangling the opportunity for more growth? Before I explain the process that many successful leaders utilize, we will revisit two of our context areas to help set the stage for our exploration.

In Chapter 1, we covered the additional context that powers the approaches, methodologies, and tools that help create the framework for the eight critical and strategic decision categories to position you and your business for success. Two of the additional context areas were "Building from the Ground Up" and "Trusting Yourself and Your Team." As you might guess, these two themes are critically important when you consider how best to build the internal infrastructure to support your business.

Recall from the Johns Hopkins University study the importance of using your childhood history of building—be it with wooden blocks, pop beads, LEGO bricks, or something else—and the resulting spatial reasoning skills that influence how you work as a "master builder" for your business today. This is how you will design and build structures from the ground up to provide a solid foundation for your business.

In addition, you need to trust your team—your business partners, your governance team, and your management team—to diligently grind through the analytical tasks and help drive your business forward. Any process that determines where the business is going that does not rely on the team expected to implement the results of the decision-making and planning is bound to be ineffective and inefficient. That process should involve discussions and questions.

Any of my business partners or the executives that I advise would tell you that I am—like many of you—extremely cost-conscious (to put it kindly). I also tend to ask a lot of questions about purpose, fit, and costs for internal infrastructure investment options. Questions like these: Why do we need to license a product? Do we not have a process or solution for that already? Do we need to hire individuals for each of these roles or could we get someone who can support multiple functions? Can we meet the goal and spend less money? Do we really need the gold-plated software platform, or is there a less robust and less costly piece of software that will meet the needs of our team?

I am always on the lookout for less costly but still viable approaches, but I am also concerned about the total cost of ownership, as you may be as well. More inquiries will follow: What are the costs for the time from our team for the less robust version of the platform? What is the timeline and what are the total costs (including product and labor) for the suggested software deployment compared to the less robust and less costly platform?

I ask these questions not simply because I am frugal or seek to have exhaustive analysis before investments are made in internal infrastructure. In fact, it is important that the analysis and time that your team spends conducting the research and assessments fit the investment you are making. If the planned investment is small, less time is likely needed to research and make the decision (and fewer questions need to be asked of your team). If the planned investment is a sizable one, however, the research and probing discussion process with your team will be well worth the time.

Many businesspeople (especially people new to a team) have an unfortunate tendency to fall prey to two types of sales pitches that will lead to more costly (than necessary) internal infrastructure investments: the hot, new platform and the top-of-the-line product. The counterweight that you will find in some organizations is the group that questions the need for the initiative: "Why do we need something new, since we have made do with what we have, and it has worked out fine so far?" Unfortunately, as you know, neither path is usually the right option, and there is usually a third way that is better. Putting effort into research, analysis, and questions is needed to get to the best outcome for your business.

Sometimes, too, the obsession with licensing or buying a software product or third-party service needs to be questioned. This is especially true when a company is growing. Sometimes internal infrastructure—in the form of processes, practices, and even tools—can get lost or be difficult for new team members to access. In short, "trust but verify" is a good rule for team discussions on internal infrastructure.

One other note of caution (I have seen this mistake made by even highly successful and entrepreneurial business leaders): Avoid, in most instances, trying to turn an internal infrastructure capability that you may perceive as a cost center into a revenue center. What does this mean? As leaders of small- and medium-sized businesses, many of us have been able to achieve great results by focusing on profitable revenue growth. Unfortunately, everything that is not a revenue and profit center can be viewed as a cost center. Some examples might be your compliance department, information security team, or other similar elements of your business. Since we are always seeking opportunities to enhance the business, many of us end up convincing ourselves that we can turn these cost centers into revenue and profit centers by selling these capabilities to other similar businesses with similar needs. While this works sometimes, more often than not the talented individuals that you hired to build the internal capabilities do not want to become revenue generators. Instead, they want to do their job of delivering services to you, your team, and your business. The results I see too often are that these valuable team members become frustrated with their role and may leave the business. And the time you spend trying to turn the cost center into a revenue and profit center would be better spent on your core business.

Twenty years of making reasonable internal infrastructure decisions (though I missed the mark on a few decisions during those decades) have taught me that while building internal infrastructure is important, having a process in place to support the analysis, decisions, and implementation related to the investments is just as significant.

The successful business leaders we surveyed support this view that growth requires infrastructure and that you need to regularize your internal operations to consistently and continually assess the need to develop internal capabilities to support your business. In fact, only 6 percent of the leaders did not have a regularized process in place for reviewing and planning for internal infrastructure to support business growth, while 94 percent had some kind of normalized plan. Of those who said they had a regular plan, 25 percent examined their infrastructure needs at least monthly, 40 percent examined their needs at least quarterly, and almost 30 percent examined their needs annually, as shown in Figure 7.1.

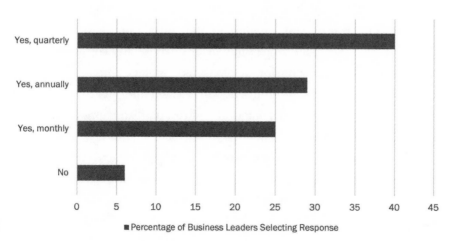

How Often Do You Revisit Business Internal Infrastructure Needs?

Figure 7.1

What are the major lessons from two decades of building internal infrastructure for small- and medium-sized businesses that can be applied to your business? There are three critically important elements: documenting everything (so you do not duplicate investments), listening to your team (but with constraints), and extending the foundation (from the ground up).

Documenting Everything (to Avoid Duplicative Investments)

Few things are as frustrating to a business leader as seeing duplicative investments being contemplated—or worse, having been made. Unfortunately, countless small- and medium-sized businesses rely on oral histories rather than thoroughly documented and disseminated processes, practices, and tools that support their own business culture.

When you experience team growth or team turnover, you will find that the oral histories are no longer viable as a method of sustaining institutional wisdom. Within many organizations that I have advised, potential solutions (such as purchasing a platform for a certain function) can often—with some internal inquiries—end up becoming moot. This happens because a process, practice, or tool already exists to meet that need, but team member changes and a lack of continuity consigned it to the intellectual property version of a long-term storage unit.

To avoid this problem (and the potential for the wasted time and resources that accompany it), one of the most pragmatic options for you as a business leader to address internal infrastructure needs is to make sure the plans for the foundation you have laid and built are actually available to your team. If you document everything, it will not just save time and resources—it will ultimately help your team execute better and drive successes for the business.

What Group Do You Engage to Revisit
Business Internal Infrastructure Needs?

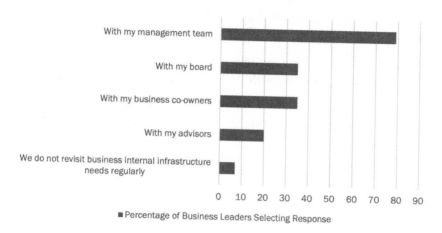

Figure 7.2

Listening to Your Team
(but with Constraints Known to All)

Since we are on the topic of your team, listening to their thoughts and needs on internal infrastructure is crucial to making the right decisions about internal infrastructure for your business. After all, you and your team are the users of the internal infrastructure that supports your business and its operations; however, you need to make sure your team has the same constraints on investment in mind that you do (and that you trust but verify their recommendations).

Recall from Chapter 2 that the first of our approaches is to use human-centered design thinking to guide the planning and actions for the business decisions you make about the future of your business. As noted earlier, as design thinking evolved, it became clear that the individuals who were going to use the products, engage the services, or work in the businesses were key figures to place at the center of the development of requirements for the products, services, and businesses.

The survey of our expert business leaders validates the value of listening to your team and making your colleagues the key players in the development of plans for business internal infrastructure. Nearly 80 percent of the executives revisit these foundational elements with their management teams, as noted in Figure 7.2. Furthermore, about 35 percent of the executives also cover this topic with their governance teams and co-owners, while 20 percent discuss these matters with advisors. Notably, only a little more than 5 percent do not revisit business internal infrastructure on any regular basis with anyone.

The best practice is to discuss internal infrastructure needs in each management team and each governance team meeting. This conclusion is validated by the results of our survey of the expert business leaders.

Based on my experience with the management teams and governance teams that I have either built or advised, you should ensure your team members are willing to voice their opinions on important topics such as:

- What is missing from the business internal infrastructure that they or their team members need to do their jobs better or deliver for customers?

- What do they believe needs to be done to support your business culture or rebuild it?

- How should investments be prioritized?

- What are the critical timelines for implementing the priorities for infrastructure investments?

It is important to note that in your management team and governance team meetings, you should provide updates on existing and currently planned internal infrastructure initiatives and results, potential resources that are available for new internal infrastructure initiatives, and scale-backs on planned internal infrastructure projects. Focusing the discussions on the investments being made, the potential for new investments, and limitations of time and money can generally ensure that overbuilding and the resulting overextension of resources do not dominate the discussions. Instead, you can have realistic and reasonable conversations—with questions and thoughtful responses—on the investments based on the existing constraints.

Extending the Foundation (from the Ground Up)

While sourcing input on infrastructure options is easy (and you likely have found that there are never shortages of suggestions), how do you make sure you make the right decisions about investing in the future of your business after you and your team have discussed the needs and priorities? You start by making decisions that focus on efficient expenditures that are aligned to the needs of the business and that do not kill your business culture. Both of these can be done by focusing on rebuilding your business the same way you built it—from the ground up.

Building the road you intend to travel along or extending the foundation for the larger structure you want to support requires discipline and the investment of time and financial resources. If you are like me and are hyper-concerned about efficiency and the potential for overextending yourself, your team, and your business, you may cringe every time the topic of spending time, money, and talent on infrastructure is discussed.

Like me, you may have made the unfortunate mistake of not investing in internal infrastructure in a timely manner. You may have placed yourself, your team, and your business in a position of not being able to support the needs of your team, your clients, or your stakeholders. If so, then you realize the importance of balancing the build-out of your business with the risks of overspending or killing the culture of your business.

Because of these risks, when you make decisions to extend your foundation, you will need to be certain that your assessment and decision-making activities are coupled with the constraints you deem appropriate—time, financial resources, and your organizational culture. And you will need to make sure all of these things align to your current and future business, not the business you had when you were bootstrapping, not taking paychecks, and maxing out your credit cards or living off your past retirement savings while you built up cash flows. Based on two decades of leading and advising small- and medium-sized businesses, two elements are important to consider when readying your business for future growth and sustainment.

For me and for many of the executive leaders I have advised, the first (and most difficult) aspect of extending the foundation is being mentally comfortable with making the investments—whether it is hiring a human resources manager to lead talent development, hiring a financial leader to guide accounting and planning, licensing a new software tool for customer relationship management or internal knowledge management, or investing in tools to help deliver services to clients. Many leaders excel at spending money and time. I do not. That is why, for me, it is important to ensure that some of the trusted members of my management team are the types of people who are process-oriented and very good at making recommendations on the expenditures that need to be made to support the growth and sustainment of the business. Such expenditures need to be reasonable and take into account our company culture and limitations on time and financial resources.

The second element of internal infrastructure development that requires special attention when moving forward with investments is aligning the internal infrastructure development to the organizational culture. This is one of the aspects I have seen many executive leaders and management team members struggle with over and over again.

I often think the ultimate goal of making internal infrastructure investments is to help your team get more done more efficiently in a manner that is compliant with laws, rules, and regulations. This is especially true in heavily regulated industries (which are becoming more and more common). Unfortunately, when internal infrastructure investments veer away from these objectives and infrastructure is created for its own sake (and not aligned to time, resources, and culture), your team may feel like they are drowning in bureaucracy. The result of this overbuilding is that key team members grow frustrated and may leave your business.

When you are making decisions about internal infrastructure and implementing those decisions, keep an eye on balancing your future with your past so you do not overbuild and lose the support of your team along the way. If your team helps you spend a little money today, but you align those expenditures to what you can afford and the culture you want to sustain and grow, you will have smooth travels ahead.

In short, make sure you rebuild and extend from the ground up the same way you built in the beginning. Invest just enough to sustain your business structure, but not so much that you never get to build on the foundation.

Applying the Blueprint

Let us look at how we apply our methodologies and tools to examine this fourth critical and strategic decision: What is the best way to build infrastructure to support growth without killing profitability or sacrificing the engines that are driving my business?

As with the prior questions we examined, we will use a fictional composite example drawn from several companies that I have led or advised. This example will show us how to apply the methodologies and tools from our blueprint to this internal infrastructure investment question. It is important to bear in mind that you likely will generate more than one card when you advance your process, and the concepts we use in this chapter are just one example to support your own activities.

Let us start our assessment phase for potential internal infrastructure investments by exploring the problems or opportunities that exist for our business such an investment could potentially address. This involves assessing the internal infrastructure needs and options. For each problem or opportunity, we ask the detailed questions related to background and context, impact on future success or failure, constraints with solving the problem or meeting the opportunity, expected benefits to solving the problem or meeting the opportunity, and options for solving the problem or meeting the opportunity. An example of this assessment phase for exploring potential internal infrastructure investment options to create the conditions for success based on our fictional company is shown in Table 7.1.

PROBLEM AND OPPORTUNITY CARD—
BUILDING INFRASTRUCTURE EXAMPLE

Problem/Opportunity Title	Internal Knowledge Management
Problem/Opportunity Summary	Our team has grown dramatically and, unfortunately, our knowledge management—in terms of domain knowledge and delivery know-how—has not scaled through the team member-to-team member "training by doing" model we used historically. As a result, our service delivery activities are not standardized across the company, and we consume too many resources, thus "reinventing the wheel" on each new client engagement. We need better knowledge management and knowledge transfer for our tools, processes, practices, and resources.
Background/Context	In our early operating history, a member of our executive founder team was engaged on each new client project. These leaders brought the institutional knowledge of the tools, processes, practices, and resources from client project to the next client project, improving along the way. Our organization is growing, and we are hiring new project leads on a regular basis. As a result, we have lost the knowledge transfer that helped our organization to deliver strong value for customers, as our projects do not have the ability to leverage all our organizational know-how in terms of tools, processes, practices, and resources.
Impact and Alignment to Future Success or Failure	Our services margins, which were comparable to industry-best, have deteriorated, and many new projects are now break-even or nominally profitable due to the lack of internal knowledge transfer to jump-start each new client engagement.
Constraints on Solving/Meeting	We cannot afford to spend significant resources on outside software to support this knowledge management and knowledge transfer. A maximum of two team members from our service delivery team are available for two calendar quarters to conduct the work; however, we may be able to make additional internal personnel time available—partially supported by client projects—to support the review of those tools, processes, practices, and resources that can support the client delivery activities. Any knowledge management and knowledge transfer portal costs must be included within current team collaboration software platform costs, as additional software costs are not viable.

Benefits of Solving/Meeting	We can regain our differentiation based on our top-tier industry know-how and help our business become more profitable again.
Options for Solving/Meeting	We need to create templates from our service delivery tools, document our processes and practices for use of the tools, and develop a resources portal to support accessing and updating of these tools and other knowledge resources by our team.
Applicable Category	Internal infrastructure development
Prioritization	High—subject to decision-making process
Status	Awaiting decision-making about prioritization

Table 7.1. Problem and Opportunity Card—Building Internal Infrastructure Example

Next, we move from analysis and conceptualization to decision-making about potential internal infrastructure investments based on available resources. We use the same two-step process to evaluate and prioritize—taking our problem and opportunity card example from Table 7.1 and determining potential planning and implementation priorities as in Table 7.2.

DECISION-MAKING STAGE-GATES—
BUILDING INTERNAL INFRASTRUCTURE EXAMPLE

Problem/ Opportunity Title	Internal Knowledge Management	
Stage-Gate #	**Questions to Answer**	**Result**
Stage-Gate 1	• Question 1: Does the problem or opportunity cause a loss of revenue, loss of profit margin, loss of employees, mis-alignment of our mission, or other potential failure? • Answer 1: Yes. Our service delivery issues and lack of profit-ability are putting our business growth and viability at risk. • Question 2: Does the solution represent an opportunity to increase revenue, margins, team stability, business alignment to mission, or future success? • Answer 2: Yes. A knowledge management initiative to ensure that our tools, processes, practices, and resources are documented and accessible to our team will help position the business for better client delivery and financial performance. • Question 3: Does the problem or opportunity merit poten-tial prioritization despite not eliciting a "yes" to one of the preceding questions? • Answer 3: Not applicable, as the answers to both Question 1 and Question 2 are "yes."	Since the answer is "yes" to the first two questions, the problem and opportunity card will be moved to decision-making stage-gate 2.
Stage-Gate 2	• Question 1: Can the problem be solved or an opportunity be seized for a reasonable investment of resources and with-in a reasonable timeline? • Answer 1: Yes, we believe that the creation of service delivery tool templates, documentation of our processes and practices for use of the tools, and development of a resources portal to help our team access and update these tools and other knowledge resources is achievable on a quick timeline with limited investment. • Question 2: Should we prioritize the solving of the problem or the seizing of the opportunity as one of our top five priori-ties to position the business for success and/or avoid failure? • Answer 2: Yes, as we risk future client satisfaction and finan-cial performance issues without addressing this need.	Since the answer is "yes" to both questions, the problem and opportunity card will be moved to planning.

Table 7.2. Decision-Making Stage-Gates—Building Internal Infrastructure Example

Our example provides a result that is a prioritized problem or opportunity; therefore, we proceed to planning by creating an initiative planning charter with each of the key elements. We will need to consider how to ensure this proposed change to create a better foundation for our business, our team, and our stakeholders takes place. Similarly, we need to ensure that implementation timeline estimates are reasonable in the context of other activities and our business culture.

An example of this planning process in action through an illustrative initiative planning charter follows in Table 7.3.

INITIATIVE PLANNING CHARTER— BUILDING INTERNAL INFRASTRUCTURE EXAMPLE

Initiative Title	Knowledge Management Platform for Service Delivery
Problem/Opportunity and Initiative Summary	Develop a knowledge management platform to ensure that our tools, processes, practices, and resources are shared and leveraged company-wide
Planning Leader	Joyce Xi
Planning Team Members	Joyce Xi Ali Kamgar Femi Osia Gabrielle Turner
Key Implementation Steps	• Develop knowledge management plan • Develop concepts for tools, documentation, resources, and portal • Validate/update concepts with service delivery team • Investigate options from team collaboration tools • Finalize plan, concepts, and timelines • Deliver knowledge management portal (including tools, processes, practices, and resources) with iterative service delivery team feedback during development

continued

Resources Needed	• Delivery team time needed for planning, validation, development, and feedback (limited to equivalent of two team members unless client delivery permits support for review) • Team collaboration platform (existing, but may need configuration)
Communications Strategy and Steps	Develop talking points for service delivery team (to solicit input and engagement for validation)
Key Implementation Timelines	• + ~15 days—Develop knowledge management plan • + ~30 days—Develop concepts for tools, documentation, resources, and portal (based on options from team collaboration tools) • + ~15 days—Validate/update concepts with service delivery team • + ~15 days—Finalize plan, concepts, and timelines • + ~45 days—Deliver knowledge management portal (including tools, processes, practices, and resources) with service delivery team iterative feedback during development

Table 7.3. Initiative Planning Charter—Building Internal Infrastructure Example

With planning complete (and hopefully approved for implementation), we move to the most critical step in the process—implementation. For this step, we use our initiative planning charter tool as a stepping stone. In doing so, we designate the leader, empower a team, delineate resources, establish an implementation monitoring protocol, develop a schedule, establish a mechanism for identifying and managing unforeseen issues and obstacles, and determine the required final activity for initial completion. As with the planning activities, we need to consider how to ensure this initiative will be positive for the company, our team members, and stakeholders. Similarly, we need to ensure the implementation charter is updated as issues and obstacles occur and adjust the dates for execution while keeping reasonable timelines.

An example of this planning process in action through an illustrative initiative implementation charter follows in Table 7.4.

INITIATIVE IMPLEMENTATION CHARTER— BUILDING INTERNAL INFRASTRUCTURE EXAMPLE

Initiative Title	Knowledge Management Platform for Service Delivery
Problem/ Opportunity and Initiative Summary	Develop a knowledge management platform to ensure that our tools, processes, practices, and resources are shared and leveraged company-wide
Implementation Leader	Joyce Xi
Implementation Team Members	Joyce Xi Ali Kamgar Femi Osia Camila Martinez Gabrielle Turner
Implementation Resources	• Delivery team time needed for planning, validation, development, and feedback (limited to the equivalent of two team members unless client delivery permits support for review) • Team collaboration platform (existing, but may need configuration)
Implementation Monitoring Protocol	• 2x weekly knowledge management team meetings • Weekly status updates during weekly management team meeting
Key Implementation Steps and Schedule	• May 1—Launch of initiative • May 15—Develop knowledge management plan • June 15—Develop concepts for tools, documentation, resources, and portal (and portal based on options from team collaboration tools) • June 30—Validate/update concepts with service delivery team • July 15—Finalize plan, concepts, and timelines • September 1—Deliver knowledge management portal (including tools, processes, practices, and resources) with service delivery team iterative feedback during development • March 1—Assessment of first six months of company service delivery activities with new knowledge management capabilities

continued

Issues/Obstacles Encountered and Resulting Implementation Plan Changes	None encountered to date (and no changes to plan)
Final Activity Required for Initial Implementation Completion	Review of impact on tools, processes, practices, resources, and portal on service delivery outcomes and profitability at six months after launch

Table 7.4. Initiative Implementation Charter—Building Internal Infrastructure Example

In this chapter, we have covered internal infrastructure development as one of the eight critical and strategic decision categories for small- and medium-sized businesses. I hope the contents of this chapter will help you as you consider how to make the decisions to build and expand core infrastructure for your business. By applying this streamlined methodology and tools, you can build a strong foundation for your business by making the right internal infrastructure investments to position your ventures for future successes.

IN REVIEW

What did we learn from this chapter?

1. To make the right internal infrastructure investments for you, your team, and your business, you need to focus on building from the ground up and trusting yourself and your team (but with verification).

2. Three key themes have helped small- to medium-sized business founders, owners, and leaders make the right internal infrastructure investments to help them achieve business successes:

   a. Documenting everything (so you do not duplicate investments)

b. Listening to your team (but with constraints known to all)

c. Extending the foundation (from the ground up)

3. One of the most pragmatic ways to address internal infrastructure needs is to make sure all the processes, practices, and infrastructure you used to build the foundation of your business are well documented and easily available to your team.

4. The most important topics for management team and governance team conversations about internal infrastructure (which should be bounded by the current financial and resource realities) are the following:

   a. What is missing from the business internal infrastructure and is needed to create the desired outcomes?

   b. What do they believe needs to be done to support your business culture or rebuild it?

   c. What do they think are priorities for investments?

   d. What do they think are the critical timelines for implementation of the infrastructure investment priorities?

5. Extending your foundations to support your future business growth and sustainment starts by making decisions that focus on efficient expenditures that are aligned to the business's needs and do not kill your business culture. Both of these can be achieved by focusing on rebuilding your business the same way you built it—from the ground up.

To help you get ready for the work you will do to examine the options for building your internal infrastructure to support growth or sustainment of your business, take a little time to answer the following four questions to help determine how to best make these investments for your business.

FOR FURTHER EXPLORATION

How do you assess the needs of your business for internal infrastructure enhancements (and how should you update this assessment model)?

_____

_____

_____

_____

What are the biggest internal infrastructure issues that you and your team believe may inhibit success?

_____

_____

_____

_____

What internal infrastructure investment constraints exist relative to these priorities?

_____

_____

_____

_____

What are the internal infrastructure items that should be the priorities for investment?

_____

_____

_____

_____

8

BREAKING THROUGH AND BREAKING UP

"When partners fall out, the ownership, control, and even survival of their company are threatened."

—PHILIP THURSTON

Unfortunately, not every team of business partners or co-owners will remain together forever. Sometimes, business owners will not be able to maintain their relationships, which means the business and its team cannot be sustained or acquired by another party or team of owners.

In your business career, have you experienced circumstances in which your business partnership or co-ownership arrangement reached the breaking point? How did you handle it? Did you and your partners have the right mindsets for approaching issues with one another? Did you and your business partners develop internal processes to help you work through difficult patches in your business relationships? Did you and your co-owners develop the necessary legal structures to support working through these conflicts? And when working through the problems did not work, did you have the legal structures in place to help you make necessary decisions?

Picking Your Partners

Selecting the "right" business partners is very important. Our survey of successful business leaders indicated that more than 45 percent of these executives had made a mistake in their professional careers by picking the "wrong" business partners. This mistake was the second most cited common error from our expert operators of small- and medium-sized businesses.

What do we mean by "picking the wrong" business partners? If we probed more deeply with this group, it is likely these business partners were not wrong in the beginning but became wrong as a result of failing to have the right mindsets, processes, and legal structures in place to support reasonable resolutions of disputes when friction arose between the business partners or when the owners decided to part ways. (I will use the terms *partners* and *partnership* in this chapter and throughout the book to equate to all types of business co-owners and co-ownership. Both terms tend to be used more regularly than other terms in everyday conversation among business leaders, regardless of the legal structure for their business.)

Many business-management thought leaders equate navigating the relationships among business partners to managing marriages and domestic partnerships. This is certainly a reasonable analogy in many ways—there is a need for communication, a need to be willing to work through disagreements, and the presence of other individuals who are impacted by the dynamics of the partners (such as children in a family or employees in a business). But managing business relationships is, at least to me, a lot more straightforward than managing personal relationships.

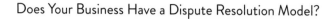

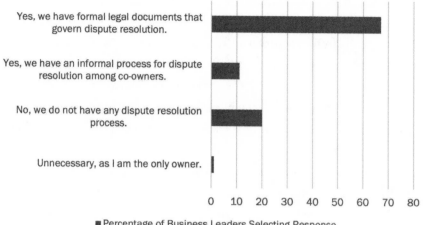

Figure 8.1

Resolving Disputes

Perhaps my legal background leads me to this conclusion, but in the United States and Canada (which are the two countries in which I have firsthand business experience), it is either a standard practice or a statutory requirement to have some type of formal legal document that defines how the owners of the business will engage in decision-making and, in some instances, how they will disassociate from one another. Some examples are bylaws and shareholder agreements for corporations, partnership agreements for legal partnerships, and operating agreements for U.S. limited liability companies. These documents are far more commonplace and (when drafted effectively) include more detailed information about communications and engagement models during difficult times or business breakups than prenuptial agreements that form the basis for marital or domestic partnership split-ups.

There is a difference between simply having these legal documents and having great versions of these documents that you and your partners use to resolve disputes and manage fractured business relationships. If you have these types of legal documents, but they do not provide formal processes for managing these business partner issues and conflicts, you should revisit their content—with competent legal counsel—and do so relatively quickly.

The results from our survey of successful business leaders validate this position. More than 67 percent of those business leaders have formal legal documents that govern dispute resolution among business partners, as shown in Figure 8.1. Meanwhile, the same survey data indicate that 33 percent of our expert business leaders lag a little on making sure their legal documents that support their decision-making and management of owner conflicts include a dispute resolution model; 20 percent lack any dispute resolution process, and 10 percent have an informal process for dispute management between co-owners.

While you may not need to have formal legal documents that include structures for dealing with difficult times and business breakups, if you put in the time early on to consider the details of these legal documents—either contemporaneously with the formation of your business or shortly thereafter before any problems start, you and your business partners will be in a better position to deal with problems and potential breakups than most marriages or domestic partnerships. Just as significantly, you will also be equipped to deal with how best to break up with your business partners, instead of tearing down your business when you end up with irreconcilable business differences.

Just as you likely have in your business lifetime, in my business career I have witnessed many talented and successful individuals who have failed to invest time developing the perspectives, plans, and legal structures that would help them manage their business versions of marriages or domestic partnerships.

The results of this lack of foresight are destructive at their worst and problematic at best. Sometimes the result is an increase in tensions during business interactions—not just between and among the business partners, but also in the presence of other team members. And those tensions lead to heightened pressures within the business. Other times, these issues lead to full-scale internal battles within the business for control of decision-making, command of the hearts and minds of teammates, and a poisoning of the business culturally.

If you have been part of these types of scenarios, you probably want to avoid them again at all costs. And if you have been fortunate enough not to have experienced them yet, you surely want to avoid these troubling experiences and the negative impacts that such conflicts can inflict on your business and your business career.

Fortunately, it is possible to break through the business disputes—even if it means breaking up with your business partners—instead of witnessing the breakdown of your business and the destruction of the business reputations and careers of you and your partners.

What are the major lessons I have learned from more than twenty years of supporting small- and medium-sized business leaders as they determined how to manage their way through difficulties in their business partnerships without killing their businesses? There are three essential components to breaking through instead of breaking down:

- Developing the right mindsets

- Agreeing on the processes

- Making sure you write down the most significant elements of your dispute resolution plans clearly and unambiguously

Mindsets for Breaking Through

The right mindset for breaking through involves your realization that—just as in a marriage or a domestic partnership—you need to have ground rules, have constant communication, and be comfortable with compromise. But your own awareness of the need for this way of thinking is not enough. There must be a shared awareness and understanding between and among the business partners.

Former Yahoo! chief executive officer and Google executive Marissa Mayer provided some great wisdom in a 2012 *Bloomberg* article about avoiding burnout. Her advice can also be applied to building resilient partnership dynamics. Mayer suggested that resentment is an underlying cause of burnout, "and you beat it by knowing what it is you're giving up that makes you resentful. . . . So, find your rhythm, understand what makes you resentful, and protect it. You can't have everything you want, but you can have the things that really matter to you."[16] Mayer went on to suggest that if you figure out what really matters to you, you will be able to sustain an intense workload for a long time.

This is a key element of establishing the shared mindsets between you and your business partners. The very first thing I recommend to founders who have started to experience tension with each another is to reset and reestablish the initial ground rule(s) about what each of the partners wants to protect. (I recommend the same thing to new founders so they can set up a strong foundation from the beginning.)

Deciding what you want to protect is difficult. It took me a long time to figure it out. The majority of my business career has been spent as a husband and a father. If you are a parent, you know how frantic the mornings before school can be—especially when your children are young. The way your mornings evolve tends to impact the way your days, and sometimes your children's days, unfold. Unfortunately, I spent way too many mornings juggling conference calls (which often required deep attention, especially during the Great Recession and its aftermath). After a while, I realized that my mental state—whether at home in the kitchen or in the car on the way to drop off the kids at school—was negatively impacting the way they started their day. At some point, I realized that what I wanted to protect was the time with my kids before their school day. I was not perfect at protecting it, but I tried. And once I started protecting (even imperfectly) that time in the morning by indicating that I really needed to avoid calls during the 7:30 a.m. to 8:30 a.m. window, it greatly reduced the stress I felt with my business partners. It also meant I could be more fully engaged with my

---

16 Marissa Mayer, "How to Avoid Burnout: Marissa Mayer," *Bloomberg*, April 12, 2012, https://www. bloomberg.com/news/articles/2012-04-12/how-to-avoid-burnout-marissa-mayer.

daughters before school and fully engaged with my business partners either before or after that time frame.

Now that my children are older, what I need to protect has changed. What you need to protect likely will be different. If you clearly establish the ground rules for engaging with your business partners, you will be a long way toward developing the mindset for communications that will allow you to break through instead of breaking down.

I have found that this opportunity to protect one thing in your life works well not just in your interactions with business partners, but also when participating in any situation that involves teamwork. This has been true all the way down to every single project team at businesses I have helped lead.

Processes for Managing the Breakthroughs

This same principle—clarity in intent and communications—is what you and your business partners need to use to establish processes for managing your businesses and business relationships. This will help you reach breakthroughs, instead of breakdowns, for your business—even if it leads to business breakups.

When I find that business partners are having difficulties, the initial questions I usually ask focus on attempting to understand what processes these partners have established for managing their relationships.

As I investigate the dynamics of the business relationships to try to rebuild a foundation for effective collaboration, I focus on a few processes: the way the partners engage each other through meetings, the regularity of the business partner meetings, the way the partners handle disputes over strategies and decision-making, and the legal structures that mandate how the disputes are resolved (sometimes with the support of the governance team). I also look at how the business partners can break up without breaking the business apart or destroying it entirely.

In most of these explorations, the tensions between the partners have impacted the frequency and tenor of their meetings in a negative way.

More stress has produced a desire for fewer meetings, and more irregular meetings have generated more stress between the business partners. In addition, in most cases, there are few, if any, rules for how disputes are handled—whether informally or formally.

I encourage business partners who have started to see their relationship breakdown to follow some pretty simple steps. It is the same advice most professional therapists provide to their clients: open up the lines of communication, establish frequent and regular times to discuss your relationship and your shared narrative, and (if needed) engage a third party (like a board member or outside advisor) to help you try to find a way to break through instead of breaking down.

Writing Dispute Resolutions Clearly and Unambiguously

This brings us to the third component—putting your agreements in writing clearly and unambiguously. After all, if you do not write these down, it can be difficult to hold each other accountable.

Often I am asked: Do we need to write down our ground rules and meeting models? I recommend that business owners write down these agreements, even if informally and even if they believe these pacts to be trivial. Putting these covenants to one another in writing, even if not in the form of a legal document, helps the business partners to be aligned and accountable to one another.

Beyond the recommendations on non-legal pacts for ground rules and meeting models, there are often legal requirements (at least in some U.S. states) that require or express a preference for legal documents that dictate how decisions are made. Most of these legal requirements do not require that you have what I would characterize as fully developed legal documents with provisions about how disputes should be resolved for businesses or how the business might survive if the business partners decide to break up.

(Based on this premise, it seems important to note that while I am an attorney licensed to practice in several U.S. jurisdictions, I am not providing legal advice to you in this book. I encourage you to seek competent legal counsel to serve you, your business partners, your business stakeholders, and your business with specific legal advice tailored to your specific circumstances.)

What is the difference between writing something down and writing something down clearly and unambiguously?

A basic set of corporate bylaws (along with a shareholder agreement), a limited liability company operating agreement, or a partnership agreement might provide you with details on who has the authority to make decisions. The agreement may also share how meetings are convened to make those decisions. The versions of these documents that feature everything written down clearly and unambiguously would also include critical elements such as what types of decisions are made by super majorities (if any), what types of decisions are major decisions (for instance, large expenditures or encumbrances) and how those decisions are made, permitted transfers of ownership, restrictions on transfers of ownership, outcomes when a business partner passes away or gets divorced, options for ownership breakups, and fair valuation methods to ensure the exits are reasonably and equitably handled by all parties (so the business can continue even if the partners cannot).

It is this deeper level of writing down the very detailed processes for making decisions, managing disputes, and breaking up that is often skipped when businesses are established. Unfortunately, it then tends to remain overlooked as businesses grow. Does this mean you need to establish buy-sell agreements and fund life insurance policies on owners to support the execution of the outcomes if an owner meets an untimely demise? Maybe, but not necessarily. That is up to you, but it is certainly an option if you want to ensure the business does not face a massive debt burden or avoid an untenable position in terms of working with heirs to the original business partners.

I encourage you to seek experienced legal counsel to support you and your business partners as you write down the rules of engagement clearly and unambiguously. These experts will help you design the processes aligned to the particular needs of you and your business partners—and then help you craft the written words that can be legally binding. They can help you and your business partners break through disputes instead of breaking down, even when you and your partners might be breaking up.

As a result of writing down the processes and decision models, when disputes arise and tempers flare, you, your business partners, and your business stand a far better chance of not breaking down and destroying the value—and the livelihoods—of you, your family, your teammates, and their families. Remember, sometimes business partners will break up, but you do not need to kill your business and the reputations of you and your business partners in the process.

Applying the Blueprint

Let us examine how we apply our methodologies and tools to examine this fifth critical and strategic decision question: How should I manage business disputes or breakups with my business partners when relationships become frayed?

As with the prior questions we examined, we will use a fictional composite example drawn from several companies that I have led or advised. This example will show us how to apply methodologies and tools from our blueprint to this internal infrastructure investment question. It is important to bear in mind that you likely will generate more than one card when you advance your process, and the concepts used in this chapter are just one example of how you can support your own activities.

Let us start our assessment phase for structures to manage business disputes and breakups by exploring the problems or opportunities that exist for our business that it could potentially address. This involves an assessment of the business dispute resolution needs, gaps that exist, and options for addressing these gaps. For each problem or opportunity, we ask the detailed questions related to background and context, impact on future success or failure, constraints and expected benefits with solving the problem or meeting the opportunity, and options for solving the problem or meeting the opportunity. An example of this assessment phase for exploring potential business dispute resolution structural options to create the conditions for success based on our fictional company is shown in Table 8.1.

PROBLEM AND OPPORTUNITY CARD— BUSINESS DISPUTES AND BREAKUPS EXAMPLE

Problem/Opportunity Title	Improving Written Legal Structures for Dispute Resolution
Problem/Opportunity Summary	Our business has a very basic set of corporate bylaws, and there are significant gaps on the details of decision-making and dispute-resolution processes.
Background/Context	We have each had prior experiences with businesses that we have co-founded devolving into business closures due to disagreements between past business partners and do not wish to experience that again.
Impact and Alignment to Future Success or Failure	If we (as co-owners) can work through disagreements in a logical manner without stress building up, we will be able to build a sustainable business.
Constraints on Solving/Meeting	We cannot spend more than $5,000 on outside legal support to help us develop better written agreements between the owners of our business.
Benefits of Solving/ Meeting	Better dispute resolution models should help to make sure we do not break the business even if we break up as business partners.
Options for Solving/ Meeting	We need to supplement our existing bylaws (with more robust, amended bylaws) and a related shareholder agreement that includes the following: what types of decisions are major decisions and how those decisions are made, what restrictions should exist on transfers of ownership, what happens if one of us gets divorced or dies, and how we deal with fair valuation methods to ensure that the exits are reasonably and equitably handled by all parties.
Applicable Category	Business Partner Dispute Resolution
Prioritization	Medium—subject to decision-making process
Status	Awaiting decision-making about prioritization

Table 8.1. Problem and Opportunity Card—Business Disputes and Breakups Example

Next, we move from analysis and conceptualization to decision-making about planning for the resolution of business owner disputes based on available resources and needs. Then we use the same two-step process to evaluate and prioritize, taking our problem and opportunity card example from Table 8.1 and determining potential planning and implementation priorities as shown in Table 8.2. The result in this scenario is that this card is the lowest ranked of our top five priorities for planning and implementation, which will impact both planning prioritization and implementation timing.

DECISION-MAKING STAGE-GATES— BUSINESS DISPUTES AND BREAKUPS EXAMPLE

Problem/ Opportunity Title	Improving Written Legal Structures for Dispute Resolution	
Stage-Gate #	Questions to Answer	Result
Stage-Gate 1	• Question 1: Does the problem or opportunity cause a loss of revenue, loss of profit margin, loss of employees, misalignment of our mission, or other potential failure? • Answer 1: Yes. If our business owners do not agree on how to continue the business if one partner desires to exit, the business might need to shut down. • Question 2: Does the solution represent an opportunity to increase revenue, margins, team stability, business alignment to mission, or future success? • Answer 2: Yes. Strong written decision-making and dispute resolution plans will help with business stability. • Question 3: Does the problem or opportunity merit potential prioritization despite not eliciting a "yes" to one of the preceding questions? • Answer 3: Not applicable, as the answers to both Question 1 and Question 2 are "yes."	Since the answer is "yes" to the first two questions, the problem and opportunity card will be moved to decision-making stage-gate 2.

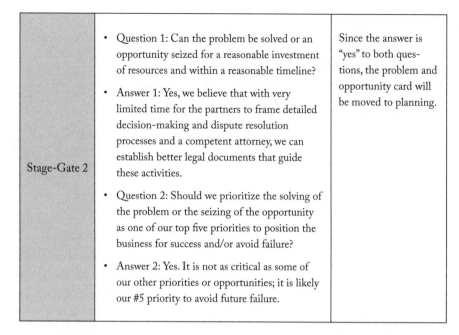

| Stage-Gate 2 | • Question 1: Can the problem be solved or an opportunity seized for a reasonable investment of resources and within a reasonable timeline?

• Answer 1: Yes, we believe that with very limited time for the partners to frame detailed decision-making and dispute resolution processes and a competent attorney, we can establish better legal documents that guide these activities.

• Question 2: Should we prioritize the solving of the problem or the seizing of the opportunity as one of our top five priorities to position the business for success and/or avoid failure?

• Answer 2: Yes. It is not as critical as some of our other priorities or opportunities; it is likely our #5 priority to avoid future failure. | Since the answer is "yes" to both questions, the problem and opportunity card will be moved to planning. |

Table 8.2. Decision-Making Stage-Gates—Business Disputes and Breakups Example

Our example provides a result that is a prioritized problem or opportunity, and we proceed to planning by creating an initiative planning charter with each of the key elements. We will need to consider how to ensure this proposed change to create a better foundation for our business, our team, and our stakeholders takes place. Similarly, we need to ensure that implementation timeline estimates are reasonable in the context of other activities and our business culture, given that this problem is not at the top of the list of our priorities.

An example of this planning process in action through an initiative planning charter follows in Table 8.3.

INITIATIVE PLANNING CHARTER— BUSINESS DISPUTES AND BREAKUPS EXAMPLE

Initiative Title	Improving Written Legal Structures for Dispute Resolution
Problem/Opportunity and Initiative Summary	Supplement our existing bylaws (with more robust amended bylaws) and a related shareholder agreement to provide details on how decision-making and dispute resolution should occur within our business
Planning Leader	Gabrielle Turner
Planning Team Members	Gabrielle Turner Javier Soto
Key Implementation Steps	• Identify and secure legal counsel to take concepts and create legal documents for our review • Develop list of agreed-upon concepts for what types of decisions are major decisions and how those decisions are made, what restrictions should exist on transfers of ownership, what happens if one of us gets divorced or dies, and how we deal with fair valuation methods to ensure that the exits are reasonably and equitably handled by all parties • Delivery of draft documents for review from legal counsel • Finalize and sign new bylaws and shareholder agreement
Resources Needed	• Executive team time needed for concept development and document review • $5,000 in outside legal expenditures
Communications Strategy and Steps	Develop talking points for governance team about initiative and their roles with planning and implementation
Key Implementation Timelines	• + ~5 days—Research, selection, and engagement of outside legal counsel • + ~5 days—Development of agreed-upon concepts for new bylaws and shareholder agreement • + ~10 days—Initial draft of documents for review by owners and governance team • + ~10 days—Finalization (by owners and governance team) and signing of new bylaws and shareholder agreement

Table 8.3. Initiative Planning Charter—Business Disputes and Breakups Example

With planning complete (and hopefully approved for implementation—albeit over a longer period of time because it is our fifth-ranked priority), we move to the most critical step in the process—implementation. Here, we rely on our initiative planning charter tool as a stepping stone. In doing so, we designate the leader, empower a team, delineate resources, establish an implementation monitoring protocol, develop a schedule, establish a mechanism for identifying and managing unforeseen issues and obstacles, and determine the required final activity for initial completion. Like the planning activities, we need to consider how to ensure this initiative will be positive for the business, our team members, and stakeholders. Similarly, we need to ensure the implementation charter is updated as issues and obstacles occur, including adjusting dates for execution while keeping reasonable timelines.

An example of this planning process in action through an initiative implementation charter—with some longer timelines based on its low prioritization compared to our other top four priorities—follows in Table 8.4.

INITIATIVE IMPLEMENTATION CHARTER– BUSINESS DISPUTES AND BREAKUPS EXAMPLE

Initiative Title	Improving Written Legal Structures for Dispute Resolution
Problem/ Opportunity and Initiative Summary	Supplement our existing bylaws (with more robust amended bylaws) and a related shareholder agreement to provide details on how decision-making and dispute resolution should occur within our business
Implementation Leader	Gabrielle Turner
Implementation Team Members	Gabrielle Turner Javier Soto
Implementation Resources	• Executive team time needed for concept development and document review • $5,000 in outside legal expenditures

continued

Implementation Monitoring Protocol	Status updates during governance team meetings
Key Implementation Steps and Schedule	• February 1 (next year)—Launch of initiative • February 6—Research, selection, and engagement of outside legal counsel • February 11—Development of agreed-upon concepts for new bylaws and shareholder agreement • February 21—Initial draft of documents for review by owners and governance team • March 3—Finalization (by owners and governance team) and signing of new bylaws and shareholder agreement
Issues/Obstacles Encountered and Resulting Implementation Plan Changes	None encountered to date (and no changes to plan)
Final Activity Required for Initial Implementation Completion	Signing of amended bylaws and shareholder agreement

Table 8.4. Initiative Implementation Charter—Business Disputes and Breakups Example

In this chapter, we explored structures for managing business disputes and breakups as one of the eight critical and strategic decision categories for small- and medium-sized businesses. I hope the ideas in this chapter help you embark on some deep thinking about dispute resolution structure options for your business. By applying this streamlined methodology and our tools, you can change the way you prepare for and act on the need for business dispute resolution and breakup structures to position your businesses for future successes.

IN REVIEW

What did we learn from this chapter?

1. Selecting the right business partners is important, but in many cases business partners were not wrong in the beginning. Rather, they became the wrong partners as a result of failing to have the right structures in place to support reasonable resolutions of disputes for business sustainment.

2. There are three essential components to breaking through business disputes instead of breaking down the business: developing the right mindsets, agreeing on the processes, and making sure you write down the most significant pieces of your dispute resolution plans clearly and unambiguously.

3. Breaking through involves your realization that—just as in a marriage or a domestic partnership—you need ground rules, constant communications, and to be comfortable with compromise. You also need to create shared awareness and understanding between and among the business partners about the ground rules and processes, including what you and your partners need to protect from encroachment by the business, if possible.

4. There is a difference between having basic legal documents to support how business decisions will be made and, in a manner that is clear and unambiguous, detailing in writing and in legal documents how disputes and difficulties may be handled. This includes what types of decisions are made by super majorities, what types of decisions are major decisions and how those decisions are made, permitted transfers of ownership, restrictions on transfers of ownership, outcomes when a business partner passes away or gets divorced, and options for ownership breakups and fair valuation methods to ensure the exits are reasonably and equitably handled by all parties.

5. When you write down—with the assistance of competent legal counsel—the rules for decision-making and dispute resolution, you, your business partners, and your business stand a far better chance of not breaking down and destroying the value of the business. As a consequence, you are less likely to destroy the livelihoods of you, your family, your teammates, and their families.

To help you get ready to develop structures for managing business disputes and breakups, it is worth contemplating the following four questions to help you determine how to establish the mindsets, processes, and written agreements for breaking through disputes between partners instead of breaking down the business.

FOR FURTHER EXPLORATION

What is your current dispute resolution plan with your business partners? What types of disputes does it allow you to address? What types of disputes are you unprepared to resolve (and what impacts could that have on your business)?

_____

_____

_____

_____

What do you want to protect from encroachment by your business (and business partners) to decrease the potential for resentment in your business relationships? Do you know what your business partners want to protect?

_____

_____

_____

_____

What other ground rules and processes should you establish to support an improved relationship and better dispute management with your business partners?

_____

_____

_____

_____

How should you enhance your business dispute resolution processes and legal documents?

_____

_____

_____

_____

9

ACTIONS FOR TRANSACTIONS

"Business opportunities are like buses,
there's always another one coming."

—RICHARD BRANSON

Some business leaders have set their sights on "doing deals" (as many of these executives and owners put it) and believe that their path to growth will involve a number of mergers and acquisitions. Other business leaders are more inclined to focus on a single deal—their eventual exit from their business—that will allow them either to retire or start their next venture. Others look at all combinations of collaboration scenarios, including investing in other businesses and divesting parts of their own businesses, as paths to business success.

In your business experiences, have you been keen on finding opportunities to acquire other companies to bolt onto your own company and create a larger, more diverse enterprise? Were you or are you interested in merging companies to add to your management team and organizational capabilities? Did you look for exit opportunities and find willing buyers for your company? Were you more interested in investing in other businesses or spinning off portions of your own business to optimize income opportunities? How did you approach these activities? Were you ready to pursue the deals when possibilities arose? Were you able to work through the processes of determining whether you would complete a transaction efficiently and avoid wasting time and resources for your business if a deal was not meant to be? Whom did you involve in these processes and analyses with you?

If you have examined opportunities for deals—which never seem to be in short supply—to grow or exit your business, or even portions of it, you likely have seen the positives and negatives that business transactions can bring. Ownership changes can help you achieve great outcomes for you, your stakeholders, your team members, and your business if you explore and act efficiently and intelligently. Conversely, if you plan to look at transaction opportunities but do not have a disciplined, systematic, and regularized process for pursuing these pathways, the chances are high that these quests become a distraction from your core business operations and put a drag on your business growth or, potentially, even the sustainability of your business.

Exploring mergers, acquisitions, exits, investments, divestments, and other deals is part of business for most of us. I cannot overstate the importance of having an organized and regularized model and a realistic view of how to use that model to explore deals and optimize the transactions you conduct.

I advise many small- and medium-sized businesses and their leaders on transactions opportunities, and I have also led businesses that ultimately were acquired by publicly traded international market leaders or merged into fast-moving roll-ups of a number of start-ups. The major difference between businesses that utilize transactions successfully and companies that do not—regardless of the type of deals being considered—comes down to their approach and how they execute their approach. The companies that leverage transactions to create successful outcomes do so in an organized and methodical way.

Back to Problems, Opportunities, and Solution Pathways

Think back to Chapter 2 and the second of the approach components from our blueprint described there—problems, opportunities, and solution pathways. This part of the approach helps us think about how we should focus on efforts during the assessment, decision-making, planning, and implementation phases of critical and strategic decisions. We have been applying this approach and the associated problem and opportunity card tool to each of our eight critical and strategic decisions. This approach is especially important to the exploration of transactions, whether mergers, acquisitions, exits, investments, divestments, or other deals. This approach is grounded in reality because it focuses on the problems you have, the opportunities you wish to seize, and the possible pathways for capitalizing on the solutions you are exploring.

We used this approach in the first business I helped found and lead for almost a decade. We analyzed our problems, opportunities, and solution pathways when the time came to assess and decide whether it was time to find a new home for our team and early Internet of Things platform technologies. We had two problems: (1) large technology companies were starting to advance make-or-buy decisions for Internet of Things platforms and (2) our business would require substantial new venture capital investment and likely a relocation of our team from Morgantown, West Virginia, to the Washington, DC, metropolitan region based on funding negotiations to compete with the leading technology companies. Our opportunities and our solution pathways arrived in the form of inbound inquiries from channel partners that wanted to integrate our team and technologies. After nearly ten years of hard work by our team, we opted for the deal that presented the best package outcomes for the team (including growth opportunities inside the new home) and our stakeholders.

What happens when you do not focus on problems, opportunities, and solution pathways? I have seen two different results in my work with strong executive leadership and governance teams. First, a tremendous amount of resources can be wasted if you and your team invest considerable time investigating, planning, and discussing transaction opportunities that end up not being pursued without first using a reasonable process to determine early on whether the opportunity is potentially a good fit. Deal fatigue among your team can be a derivative of this first outcome and a danger in its own right when your team looks at too many transaction opportunities without a clear model for how to evaluate and prioritize the options. Second, when you do not have a structured approach to assessing the suitability of potential deals from the outset, you may end up diving into the first deals you see instead of ones that are most optimal for your business and your team.

What happens when you take a more structured approach that focuses on problems, opportunities, and solution pathways in the form of potential deals? You are much more likely to find the right activities to pursue. That initial analysis will put you on the right road to pursue transactions that ought to be done. And when that happens, the processes of evaluation, deal execution, and integration seem to flow smoothly.

Preparing Through Processes

While doing deals is exciting to many business owners and executives, the reality is that you need to be prepared—in an organized way—to assess the viability of the opportunities that you find or that find you. Our survey of expert leaders validated this view. A slim majority of 54 percent indicated they have processes for assessing investments, divestments, and mergers and acquisitions, as indicated in Figure 9.1. Furthermore, 38 percent of this group indicated they only examined these types of transactions when opportunities were presented to them. A smaller number—16 percent—have a regular and structured process for examining these types of buying, selling, and investment opportunities. On the other hand, 44 percent did not have a regularized process for investments, divestments, and mergers and acquisitions activities, and an exceedingly small number—2 percent—took irregular approaches to transaction opportunities.

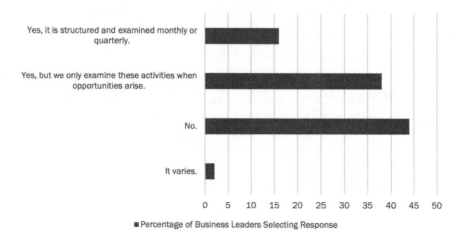

Does Your Business Have a Process for Analyzing
Investments, Divestments, Mergers, and Acquisitions?

Figure 9.1

During the past twenty years, I have advised a range of companies, from publicly traded companies to newly funded start-ups, and founded and led multiple companies that found their exit transactions through acquisitions and mergers activities or other types of transactions. The companies that successfully explored and judiciously completed transactions differ from less successful companies in their approach, their preparation, and their execution.

What are the key takeaways from two decades of advising and leading small- and medium-sized businesses as they explore a suite of transaction possibilities such as mergers, acquisitions, exits, investments, divestments, and other deals? There are three essential elements you must master to ensure that transaction opportunities benefit you and your businesses, instead of derailing your momentum and trajectory:

1. Get your business organized and ready

2. Be rational and collaborative in your pursuits

3. Understand that timing really is everything

Get Organized and Ready

As noted in the beginning of this chapter, nearly all of us who lead or help lead companies have an interest in engaging in transactions such as mergers, acquisitions, exits, investments, divestments, and other deals. We likely all have a hardwired preference for the types of deals we pursue. Serial entrepreneurs are often focused on building for an exit since our attention spans may be too short to continue with the same platform for five or ten years. Others are keen to look at ways to diversify their own business through either acquisitions or investments. The most disciplined among us are self-aware enough to consider divesting certain business lines or businesses depending on how our core business is growing and evolving.

The key—no matter what types of transactions you find yourself drawn to explore—is to be organized and ready before, during, and after transactions occur. What does this mean?

First, you need to keep your proverbial house in order to support due diligence activities related to any potential transaction. The lawyer in me believes the first step is to make sure that your own business records and files are ready in case the transaction opportunity is an acquisition of your company, a merger with another business, or a divestment of a subsidiary or line of business. Your transaction will go more quickly, and there will be less potential for due diligence findings to derail your transaction and squander your time and money in an ultimately fruitless negotiation. Essential records are the legal documents and operational documents for the business. The legal documents include your organizing documents, governing documents, ownership documents, legal filings, and all necessary records associated with the legal operations of the business. Operating documents include organizational charts, financing arrangements, contracts, intellectual property documents, litigation documents, biographies and résumés, employment files, financial records, tax records, real estate files, inventories and assets, insurance information, and competitive and strategic business analyses reports. The good news is that these activities will actually help you operate and maintain your business better—with or without any future transactions.

Second, you need to have a very detailed list ready to support your due diligence of potential merger partners, potential acquisition targets, and other businesses you may invest in. This list likely includes the same legal documents and operational documents that you use to ensure that your records are up-to-date and ready for potential deal opportunities.

I have seen deals die as a result of an inability to share standard due diligence information in a logical way. In such cases, the real issue is that the business was not being operated effectively and efficiently due to its lack of organization and structure, which resulted in the inability to share the necessary data.

(Again, it seems important to note that while I am a licensed attorney, I am not providing legal advice to you in this book. I encourage you to seek legal counsel to serve you and your business with advice on the appropriate documents needed for you to be ready for due diligence activities related to potential transactions.)

Third, it is important to look at transactions in an organized and methodical way. To do so, you and your team can develop a list of what types of transactions you are targeting. The list should include details on the criteria (such as strategic, financial, cultural, locational, synergistic, and other factors) for evaluating potential opportunities and whether potential candidates fit your criteria.

As you might have guessed, our problems, opportunities, and solutions pathway approach and our associated problem and opportunity card tool help make this a pretty straightforward process for both designing your organized structure and applying it. The result is that you have a great model and preliminary assessment that will feed your potential transaction due diligence process and decision-making opportunities, as well as your plans to line up more transaction opportunities that meet your targeted goals.

Finally, if you plan to acquire or facilitate mergers, it is important to develop a standard structure for an integration plan. This plan should focus on the who, what, and how for integrations of legal entities, personnel, operations, information technology and systems, human resources functions, accounting and finance activities, sales and marketing activities, and product or service capabilities (if such assets exist), among others. It should also heavily focus on ensuring that communications are clear from the beginning about the roles and responsibilities for the integration work and the newly expanded and united business, and communication should be sustained throughout the integration process.

Unfortunately, too often the transactions that seem most promising can be undermined by a lack of foresight on the alignment and integration of the consolidated organization. I have witnessed executives of acquired businesses that became part of heavily regulated industries assume that their post-acquisition freedom would be similar to their pre-acquisition autonomy. When this did not occur, it caused serious cultural consequences for the business, the need for continual resetting of operational models, and difficult dynamics within its leadership team for many years.

Be Rational and Collaborative

In addition to getting organized and ready, you need to be rational and collaborative in your assessment, decision-making, planning, and implementation activities related to transaction activities. We will explore both components: rational thinking and collaborative exploration.

When you are examining transaction opportunities, there is a tendency to get excited about doing the deal and get a little too attached to completing the mission. If you are looking at acquiring another business, the deal may become more and more compelling—at least in your own mind—with each passing day. If you are presented with an unexpected opportunity to sell your business, it may seem a little sad to consider ending your run, no matter how lucrative the offer or how dire the circumstances. Sometimes, too, we might fall in love with the theory of a transaction opportunity that is unlikely to exist. Thus, it is important not to become too emotional, sentimental, or optimistic when examining transaction opportunities.

The good news for most of us, provided you have built (or intend to build) a strong governance team and a strong management team, is that you do not need to go it alone. You may recall from Chapter 1 that one of the additional context themes that will help you develop a more holistic perspective in your business ventures is to trust yourself and your team. This will be helpful when you are examining transaction opportunities, engaging your business co-owners, governance board members, and management team members to help moderate some of your tendencies or emotions.

The expert business leaders we surveyed follow this premise. Only about 25 percent of these executives do not review investments, divestments, and mergers and acquisitions with some of their team members regularly, as shown in Figure 9.2. Of the approximately 75 percent that do regularly visit transaction opportunities with their teammates, nearly 50 percent review the options with their board, almost 45 percent engage their management team, more than 30 percent work with their business co-owners, and more than 25 percent collaborate with their advisors. (For this question, these leaders were allowed to select more than one option in their response.)

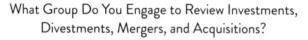

What Group Do You Engage to Review Investments, Divestments, Mergers, and Acquisitions?

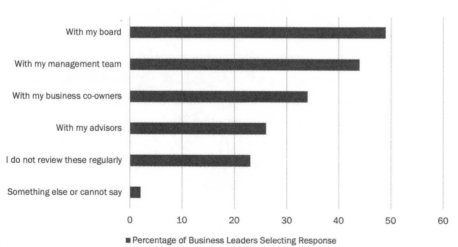

Figure 9.2

Timing Really Is Everything

This brings us to the third element—and if you have been involved in transactions previously, you likely have seen it, heard it, or lived it: Timing really is everything.

Timing is important on both sides of a transaction in mergers and acquisitions activities in terms of sequencing, market timing, pace, and your own mental state. First, this means the transaction activities need to be sequenced so each business can focus its resources on assessing, deciding, planning, and integrating without disrupting the flow of the business. Second, it is important that the activities predate the market opportunity so that the newly united enterprise can capture the full potential of the deal, rather than miss the market window.

In addition, you must ensure that you operate your transaction processes efficiently, but without rushing activities. If your pace is off, it likely will negatively impact the operations and performance of the businesses that are engaged in the potential transaction, as it consumes too much time and resources. It will also potentially put the businesses in a position of missing the market opportunity.

Finally, if you are looking for an exit from your business, it is important that you do not wait until you are completely burned out. If you wait too long, you may find that you are doing the deal to try to get out of your valley of utter exhaustion rather than because it will generate the best return for you, your co-owners, and your team members.

The result of developing an organized and regularized model for considering potential transactions—including mergers, acquisitions, exits, investments, divestments, and other deals—is that you and your business will have a road map and reasonable framework for evaluating the pathways that you find or that find you. In doing so, you will ensure that you are not just doing deals but entering into the best transactions at the optimal times to the benefit of you, your partners, your team, and your businesses.

Applying the Blueprint

It is time to apply our methodologies and tools to examine this sixth critical and strategic decision question: Should I examine opportunities to advance an acquisition of a partner or competitor, merge with a partner or competitor, sell my business, divest a part of my business, or make a new investment to help my business (and when should I do it)?

As with the prior questions we examined, we will use a fictional composite example drawn from several companies I have led or advised. This example will show us how to apply the methodologies and tools from our blueprint to this business transaction opportunities question. It is important to bear in mind that you will likely generate more than one card when you advance your process, and the concepts that we use in this chapter are just one example of how you can support your own activities.

Let us start our assessment phase for potential transaction opportunities—including mergers, acquisitions, exits, investments, divestments, and other deals—by exploring the problems or opportunities that exist for our business that a transaction could potentially address. For each problem or opportunity, we ask the detailed questions related to background and context, impact on future success or failure, constraints, and expected benefits with solving the problem or meeting the opportunity, and options for solving the problem or meeting the opportunity. An example of one outcome from this assessment phase for exploring potential business transaction options to create the conditions for success based on our fictional company is shown in Table 9.1.

PROBLEM AND OPPORTUNITY CARD—
BUSINESS TRANSACTION OPTIONS EXAMPLE

Problem/Opportunity Title	Transaction Opportunity Processes and Model
Problem/Opportunity Summary	Our business does not have a way to look at transactions in an organized and methodical way.

continued

Background/Context	We believe that consolidation will take place in our industry in the years ahead, and we want to be an acquirer rather than a target for acquisition.
Impact and Alignment to Future Success or Failure	If we have an organized model for our potential merger and acquisition opportunities, we can execute better and create a stronger, more robust business during the consolidation.
Constraints on Solving/Meeting	We cannot allow the solving of this problem and opportunity to distract us from our other higher-priority initiatives.
Benefits of Solving/Meeting	If we are more organized about pursuing transaction opportunities, we will end up with better resource allocation and results.
Options for Solving/Meeting	We need to establish a process and model for exploring transactions opportunities, including developing and maintaining a list of what types of transactions we are seeking to target, details on the criteria for evaluating the potential opportunities that fit these types of deals, a list of what candidates fit these types of transactions, and a list of our views on alignment to support prioritization of potential acquisition opportunities.
Applicable Category	Transactions
Prioritization	Medium—subject to decision-making process
Status	Awaiting decision-making about prioritization

Table 9.1. Problem and Opportunity Card—Business Transaction Options Example

Next, we move from analysis and conceptualization to decision-making about planning for the capture of business transaction options based on our prioritization of problems, opportunities, and solution pathways. Then we use the same two-step process to evaluate and prioritize, taking our problem and opportunity card example from Table 9.1 and determining potential planning and implementation priorities as shown in Table 9.2. The result in this scenario is that this card does not rank in the top five priorities for planning and implementation. This means we will likely defer both planning prioritization and implementation timing.

DECISION-MAKING STAGE-GATES— BUSINESS TRANSACTION OPTIONS EXAMPLE

Problem/ Opportunity Title	Transaction Opportunity Processes and Model	
Stage-Gate #	Questions to Answer	Result
Stage-Gate 1	• Question 1: Does the problem or opportunity cause a loss of revenue, loss of profit margin, loss of employees, misalignment of our mission, or other potential failure? • Answer 1: Yes. If we have an organized model for our potential merger and acquisition opportunities, we can execute better and create a stronger, more robust business in the years ahead. • Question 2: Does the solution represent an opportunity to increase revenue, margins, team stability, business alignment to mission, or future success? • Answer 2: Yes. A strong process and models for exploring transactions will help us with revenue growth, margins, and future successes during industry consolidation. • Question 3: Does the problem or opportunity merit potential prioritization despite not eliciting a "yes" to one of the preceding questions? • Answer 3: Not applicable, as the answers to both Question 1 and Question 2 are "yes."	Since the answer is "yes" to the first two questions, the problem and opportunity card will be moved to decision-making stage-gate 2.

continued

| Stage-Gate 2 | • Question 1: Can the problem be solved or an opportunity seized for a reasonable investment of resources and within a reasonable timeline?

• Answer 1: Yes, we believe that with very limited time, we can establish a process and model to guide these activities.

• Question 2: Should we prioritize the solving of the problem or the seizing of the opportunity as one of our top five priorities to position the business for success and/or avoid failure?

• Answer 2: No, this problem/opportunity is not as critical as our existing top five priorities (as these top five will help us become a stronger business and ready for acquisitions), but it is certainly in our top ten priorities. | Since the answer is "no" to one of our questions, the problem and opportunity card will be moved to lower-priority planning and advanced only as our higher-priority initiatives process through planning and implementation. |

Table 9.2. Decision-Making Stage-Gates—Business Transaction Options Example

Our example provides a result that is a second-tier problem or opportunity (i.e., not one of our five highest priorities), but it is one of our top ten problems and opportunities. According to our methodology, we could, as time permits, proceed to planning by creating an initiative planning charter with each of the key elements. We will need to consider how to ensure this proposed change to create a better foundation for our business, our team, and our stakeholders occurs. Similarly, we need to ensure that implementation timeline estimates are reasonable in the context of other activities and our business culture, given that this problem is not one of our highest priorities. An example of this planning process in action through an initiative planning charter follows in Table 9.3.

INITIATIVE PLANNING CHARTER—
BUSINESS TRANSACTION OPTIONS EXAMPLE

Initiative Title	Transaction Opportunity Processes and Model
Problem/ Opportunity and Initiative Summary	Establish a process and model for exploring transaction opportunities, including developing and maintaining a list of what types of transactions we are seeking to target, details on the criteria for evaluating the potential opportunities that fit these types of deals, a list of what candidates fit these types of transactions, and a list of our priorities for transaction opportunities
Implementation Leader	Grace Chang
Implementation Team Members	Gabrielle Turner Javier Soto Grace Chang Camila Martinez Sean Williams
Key Implementation Steps	• Develop a draft high-level process and model for exploring transaction opportunities • Finalize initial process and model for exploring transaction opportunities • Develop a list of what types of transactions we are seeking to target • Create criteria for evaluating the potential opportunities that fit these types of deals • Develop a list of what candidates fit these types of transactions • Develop a list of potential transaction priorities • Finalize complete process, model, and initial list of priorities

continued

Resources Needed	Time for the management team to develop the process, model, and details and to apply the process, model, and details
Communications Strategy and Steps	Develop talking points for governance team about the initiative and their roles with planning and implementation
Key Implementation Timelines	+ ~5 days—Develop a draft high-level process and model for exploring transaction opportunities + ~10 days—Finalize initial process and model for exploring transaction opportunities + ~2 days—Develop a list of what types of transactions we are seeking to target + ~5 days—Create criteria for evaluating the potential opportunities that fit these types of deals + ~5 days—Develop a list of what candidates fit these types of transactions + ~15 days—Develop a list of potential transaction priorities + ~5 days—Finalize complete process, model, and initial list of transaction opportunity priorities with management team + ~10 days—Review and approve list of transaction opportunity priorities by governance team

Table 9.3. Initiative Planning Charter—Business Transaction Options Example

With planning complete (albeit at some point in the future since this was not one of our five highest priorities), we move to the most critical step in the process: implementation. We rely on our initiative planning charter tool to help us jump-start the process. Whenever we decide that we should move to implementation, we designate the leader, empower a team, delineate resources, establish an implementation monitoring protocol, develop a schedule, establish a mechanism for identifying and managing unforeseen issues and obstacles, and determine the required final activity for initial completion. As with the planning charter, we need to consider how to ensure this initiative will be positive for the business, our team members, and stakeholders. Similarly, we need to ensure the implementation charter is updated as issues and obstacles occur, including adjusting dates for execution while keeping reasonable timelines.

An example of this planning process in action through an initiative implementation charter with some very distant timelines based on its later start given its lower priority level is shown in Table 9.4.

INITIATIVE IMPLEMENTATION CHARTER— BUSINESS TRANSACTION OPTIONS EXAMPLE

Initiative Title	Transaction Opportunity Processes and Model
Problem/ Opportunity and Initiative Summary	Establish a process and model for exploring transaction opportunities, including developing and maintaining a list of what types of transactions we are seeking to target, details on the criteria for evaluating the potential opportunities that fit these types of deals, a list of what candidates fit these types of transactions, and a list of our priorities for transaction opportunities
Implementation Leader	Grace Chang
Implementation Team Members	Gabrielle Turner Javier Soto Grace Chang Camila Martinez Sean Williams
Implementation Resources	Time for the management team to develop process, model, and details, as well as apply this process, model, and details
Implementation Monitoring Protocol	Status updates during management team and governance team meetings

continued

Key Implementation Steps and Schedule	• June 1 (next year)—Launch of initiative • June 6—Develop a draft high-level process and model for exploring transaction opportunities • June 16—Finalize initial process and model for exploring transaction opportunities • June 18—Develop a list of what types of transactions we are seeking to target • June 24—Create criteria for evaluating the potential opportunities that fit these types of deal • June 30—Develop a list of what candidates fit these types of transactions • July 15—Develop a list of potential transaction priorities • July 20—Finalize complete process, model, and initial list of transaction opportunity priorities with management team • July 30—Review and approve list of transaction opportunity priorities by governance team
Issues/Obstacles Encountered and Resulting Implementation Plan Changes	None encountered to date (and no changes to plan)
Final Activity Required for Initial Implementation Completion	Review and approve list of transaction opportunity priorities by governance team

Table 9.4. Initiative Implementation Charter—Business Transaction Options Example

In this chapter, we explored ways to consider transaction opportunities as one of the eight critical and strategic decision categories for small- and medium-sized businesses. Ideally, this content will help you do a better job of examining transaction opportunities such as acquisitions, mergers, and exits for your own business. By applying this streamlined methodology and our tools, you can change the way you consider and act on potentially promising business transaction opportunities to position your ventures for future successes.

IN REVIEW

What did we learn from this chapter?

1. The major difference between businesses that utilized transactions successfully and companies that did not—regardless of the type of deals done—comes down to their approach and how they executed their approach. The companies that leveraged transactions to create successful outcomes did so in an organized and methodical way that was informed by problems, opportunities, and solution pathways.

2. There are three essential elements you must master to ensure that transaction opportunities benefit you and your businesses instead of potentially derailing your momentum and trajectory:

    a. Getting your business organized and ready

    b. Being rational and collaborative in your pursuits

    c. Understanding that timing really is everything

3. Getting organized and ready means having the legal documents and operational documents for your business up-to-date and in good order, having a detailed list to support your due diligence activities of potential deals, developing a model to look at transactions in an organized and methodical way, and—if you plan to be an acquirer—creating a standard structure for an integration plan.

4. Being rational and collaborative in your assessment, decision-making, planning, and implementation activities related to transaction activities means not becoming too emotional, sentimental, or optimistic when examining transaction opportunities. It also means engaging your business partners and governance board members in the process.

5. Timing, in terms of sequencing, market timing, pace, and your own mental state, really is everything when it comes to

transaction opportunities. This includes mergers, acquisitions, exits, investments, divestments, and other deals.

To help you get ready for the business transaction process work you will be doing in the near future, you can consider the following four questions to help you determine how to develop an organized and regularized model for considering potential transactions that will create beneficial outcomes for you, your partners, your team, and your businesses.

FOR FURTHER EXPLORATION

How do you approach exploring potential transaction opportunities today?

_____

_____

_____

_____

What problems and opportunities exist for your company that could involve transactions of some type?

_____

_____

_____

_____

What types of transaction options are your priorities (and why)? What businesses do you envision being involved in these transactions (and why)?

_____

_____

_____

_____

What additional steps could you take to be more prepared for your target transaction opportunities?

_____

_____

_____

_____

10

WHEN DISASTER STRIKES

"When we rebuild a house, we are rebuilding
a home. When we recover from disaster,
we are rebuilding lives and livelihoods."

—SRI MULYANI INDRAWATI

If your business career coincides with mine, you likely have been part of navigating two global financial and life-impacting disasters—the Great Recession and COVID-19. If you started your business journey before me, you may also have experienced the difficulties that impacted businesses and lives when the dot-com bubble burst or the terrorist attacks occurred on September 11, 2001. Even if you are relatively new to leading your own business, you likely have seen the continuing impacts of COVID-19. Or, if you are reading this book well after its publication, you have probably experienced the effects of the latest catastrophic event that knocked our lives and businesses off their normal trajectories. In addition to these global events, there is no shortage of other impacts, such as top personnel leaving your team, natural disasters (like floods, hurricanes, and fires), cybersecurity hacks, supply chain problems, or sudden health crises, to name a few. Any of these scenarios may have presented significant issues and obstacles for you and your business. And, most likely, they felt like disasters.

When these global, local, or personal disasters struck, were you ready to face them and mitigate the damage to your business? Had you assessed the potential for these disasters to occur, and did you have plans in place to deal with them? If so, how did you work to identify these risks and develop your plans to mitigate them? When you made plans for managing through crises, did you have a way to update these response and mitigation plans?

If you have worked through a disaster, managed the crisis, and emerged on the other side or come face-to-face with a catastrophe like losing your business and having to start over again, you probably understand the need to consider potential disasters and make a plan for how to mitigate these troubles. But the question is: How prepared should you be?

Only you and your team know the right answer to how prepared you and your team should be for the potential disasters that might befall your business. If you have embraced the concept of supplementing your personal context with the additional context elements that fuel our approaches, you may find that a little more productive worrying could be an asset to you and the future of your business.

Disaster Planning as a Work in Progress

While worrying—in general—is something my mind tends to do, I have worked hard to train myself to worry productively. That means I focus on the right things to be concerned about and think through plans to manage and mitigate the risks.

Early in my business career, I worried about the basics:

- How to make sure we could cover payroll for our team if customer payments were delayed

- How to make sure we had the ability to replace me and our other business leaders if we met an untimely demise, (this was during a time when we were working at below-market salaries as we grew the business)

- How to replace our business assets if a fire or theft occurred

To address these concerns, we secured lines of credit, key person insurance, and standard business insurance coverages. As the years passed, the potentially disastrous risks that seemed important to consider and manage and mitigate—to the extent possible—became slightly more complex. Worries grew to include being sued by clients if our software did not perform as expected or our services failed to produce their contractually required outcomes. Eventually, concerns included potential litigation by acquirers if representations and warranties in transaction documents failed to be correct (despite our best efforts to ensure these pledges were accurate). We loaded up on more insurance, such as errors and omissions, cybersecurity, and even the obscure representations and warranties coverages.

Worrying about risks and mitigating these specters through traditional and even obscure business insurance is obviously a very important baseline risk mitigation activity (even if the representations and warranties coverage might have been a very expensive bit of overkill, as our deal covenants proved to be correct). But far more preparation is required to be ready when disaster strikes in the form of customer attrition, loss of talented team members, localized natural disasters, or other catastrophes. We developed models to diversify sales channels and customers, provided stock options and other incentive opportunities to talented team members, and set up a second technology development center halfway across the U.S. Still, we always worried that we were not approaching identification and management of risks from a holistic perspective. That worry changed as I worked with businesses in industries with some firm requirements for disaster response planning.

Business Continuity Management

I have been fortunate enough to help lead and advise companies in many heavily regulated industry sectors, including defense and aerospace, energy, and banking and finance. If you are thinking that very few people ever say "fortunate" about heavy doses of government oversight, you are probably correct; however, one particular set of government requirements helped generate the principles that I recommend businesses use to be ready for when disasters strike.

The government oversight model that helped evolve my thinking about planning for disasters came in the form of the *Federal Financial Institution Examination Council Information Technology Examination Handbook*.[17] I saw how the financial system regulators applied the portion of this examination handbook related to business continuity management. (Previously, this was referred to as business continuity planning until the policymakers realized that planning was only part of the puzzle.)

What does this mean for you? In the following paragraphs, I provide a brief explanation of some important background facts for our study of disaster planning options, which will help us build better foundations for the futures of our businesses.

In the U.S., the federal government has enacted laws, regulations, policies, and procedures to help ensure that the nation's privately owned banks and other financial institutions that hold cash deposits for customers are being operated safely and effectively to maintain the stability of the financial system and services to customers. In a number of areas, multiple federal organizations have oversight responsibilities for different types of financial institutions. These organizations have put together common guidance for banks and similar businesses to support the establishment and maintenance of better processes and standardized supervision. One of these areas—business continuity management—relates to the ability of these banks to maintain services for customers when disasters strike.

---

17   *Federal Financial Institution Examination Council Information Technology Examination Handbook*,
     https://ithandbook.ffiec.gov/it-booklets/business-continuity-management.aspx.

Compliance with this requirement for banks and other financial institutions means that these businesses need to identify potential disasters and threats that could impact critical functions, determine the likelihood of occurrence, assess the potential impacts, develop business continuity plans with associated processes to provide sustained services and restoration of normal operations when disasters and threats materialize, exercise and test these plans, and update both the risks and plans regularly in consultation with the entity's governance team. The goal, as you might expect, is to ensure that each financial institution meets the needs of its customers and that, in aggregate, the banking system stays stable regardless of the types of impacts it faces from natural disasters, cybersecurity impacts, and other issues.

The requirements placed on banks and financial institutions to review and conduct tests of these plans and processes on a quarterly basis is probably excessive for your business (unless you happen to be in a business that provides critical infrastructure services). But the basic model provided in the banking examination handbook mentioned previously is a great guide for all businesses to follow when building a stronger business.

Before we dive into the concepts, we will look at how this premise of developing plans for disasters in an organized manner aligns with the way that our surveyed group of business expert leaders approach this building block for their organizations. When we asked the group, only 1 percent responded that they had no organized process for preparing for disasters. A larger number—36 percent—noted they planned for responses to disasters as the problems unfolded. Conversely, a strong 58 percent indicated they had some plans for certain types of disaster management but were not ready with plans for everything. These results are shown in Figure 10.1. Also, 16 percent of the best-prepared leaders (which overlapped with the group that said they had some disaster response plans) responded that they had a formal process for assessing potential disasters and documenting plans for disaster response and management (despite not being in the banking industry where they would be required to do so).

How Do You Plan for Managing Disasters?

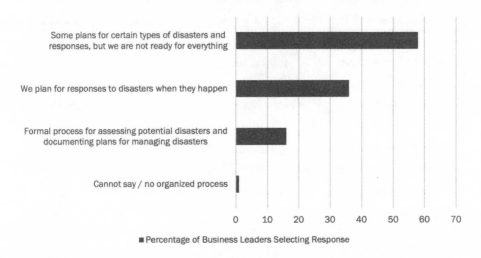

Figure 10.1

Based on the lessons learned from observing government-directed business continuity management and nearly a decade of tailoring the process to create a more streamlined model suitable for small- and medium-sized businesses, what lessons can be applied to your business? Three themes are important as you determine how prepared you should be:

1. Identify, assess, and prioritize potential disasters and risks

2. Develop response and mitigation plans for the potential disasters and risks

3. Review, experience, and update the disaster assessments and plans

Potential Disasters and Risks

You may have already identified and planned responses to at least some of the disasters that might befall you and your business. Perhaps you are sensitive to your potential business liabilities (and maybe your related potential personal liabilities as an officer and director) and have secured various types of business liability insurance. Maybe you are concerned about you or other leaders passing away and have obtained key person insurance. Or you may be concerned about losing electrical power and have purchased a backup power generator.

But have you comprehensively identified, assessed, and prioritized the potential disasters and risks that exist for your business?

We can take a cue from the banking regulatory scheme without over-burdening ourselves with its very time-consuming approach (unless, of course, you happen to be in the banking sector). We can combine the banking approach with the lessons learned from a decade of helping businesses apply the logic of the financial institution protective measures to their own activities. In this way, we can create a model to identify, assess, and prioritize potential disasters and risks that generates results but does not require more time than you are inclined to invest.

Since trusting yourself and your team is a major premise of our framework, this process is usually conducted by the management team. The governance team usually reviews the management team's analysis.

The process starts with you and your management team conducting a thorough review of potential disasters and risks that could impact critical business functions or business outcomes. To make sure this review is comprehensive, I recommend that the team explore several types of disasters and risks: natural events, technical events, malicious activity, talent issues, and business delivery issues, among others.

The next step in the process is to do some scenario planning to understand which disasters and impacts are interdependent or causally related. The following step is to estimate the likelihood and impact of each disaster or risk. Finally, the disasters and risks should be prioritized based on the combination of their impact and likelihood.

The end result should be a comprehensive and prioritized list of disasters and risks, their interrelationships, the likelihood of their occurrence, and an assessment of their potential impacts. This will allow you to work on your continuity and mitigation plans.

Response and Mitigation Plans

With this prioritized list of disasters and risks, the management team can develop plans for disaster response, mitigation, and management. Such plans should include planning for continuity or resumption of operations for each of the disasters and risks, beginning with the prioritized list.

The core of this plan will require some up-front investment and planning, including training key personnel so they are ready to fill critical roles when other key personnel are absent, implementing technology backup and restoration measures, establishing remote work options, establishing secondary operations centers, identifying alternative suppliers, and other tasks. Most importantly, you need to be as thorough as possible so the plans are actionable and can support effective responses when disasters strike.

When you develop response and mitigation plans that you know will require planning and investment, it is important to make sure the plans can be implemented and will ensure operational continuity if and when disasters strike or risks are realized. Also, you need to ensure you have clear communications plans for all of the planned response activities to support easy messaging to your team, customers, and partners.

Being aware of potential disasters and having plans to manage these issues before problems arise has obvious advantages. The same approach can help you thoughtfully manage the crisis in front of you today.

I have found it helpful to follow the same process when the multiple businesses that I help support were faced with urgent threats, especially during the early days of the COVID-19 pandemic. The major components—in times of exigent circumstances—are how to deploy talent, technology, operational activities, third-party support, and the critical communications plans that get your message out to your team, customers, and partners about the issues and how you are handling the response.

Review, Experience, and Update

Another key insight from the U.S. financial system regulators is that sometimes unanticipated disasters arrive, and you need to be as prepared as possible. The method employed by the banking system regulators for solving this problem (testing your plans through full-scale exercises, partial drills, and tabletop activities) is likely a bit too much of an expenditure of time and resources for your business (unless you happen to operate a bank). But you should certainly review and update your plans based on thoughtful reflection on changes in risks, changes in your mitigation plans, and your current operational experiences.

In terms of reviews, you likely will want to regularize these reevaluations with your team members—perhaps twice yearly or as circumstances warrant. This is much less frequent than the quarterly testing the banking examiners require of the entities they supervise, but it is more than frequent enough for most businesses to ensure that new risks can be factored into disaster response planning.

You should update your list of potential disasters and your plans for managing these obstacles as you operate your business and experience life. Sometimes the struggles of daily life offer the best opportunities to identify potential disasters and ways to mitigate their impacts. For instance, I had a personal disaster that could have become a catastrophe for my business in 2017. In fact, the event actually helped prepare me for remote work, which was very fortuitous when COVID-19 appeared. Here is the story.

Although I had never intended to coach any youth sports, I ended up being asked to coach my younger daughter's basketball team. Because of this, I found myself—unfortunately—actively engaged in instructional demonstrations. After a couple of crossovers and cuts too many (and too many years after switching from soccer to running, which did not involve these dynamic movements), I was down on the ground feeling like something in my lower leg had exploded. My orthopedist confirmed that I had completely ruptured my Achilles tendon, and I scheduled a surgical repair a week later. I did not see this physical disaster coming—nor did I know the impact it would have for the business when I was out of the office for three solid weeks and unable to do any business travel for nearly three months. We were able to shift all of the work activities to online meetings and did not see a drag on our productivity, output, or sales results. I cannot say I enjoyed the surgery or the rehabilitation, but it did make the transition to fully remote work during the COVID-19 pandemic quite seamless, since I knew that remote work was not only possible but could sometimes be more efficient if managed well.

Combining a review of current risks with the reality of your experiences will allow you to have the information you need to update your plans and ensure that you stay well prepared for as many disasters as you can envision unfolding.

How prepared should you be? As prepared as you, your management team, and your governance team decide that you should be. In most cases, that means you will be a little more prepared and maybe a little more formalized with your disaster preparedness activities than you and your business are today.

Applying the Blueprint

Let us look at how we apply our methodologies and tools to examine this seventh critical and strategic decision question: What disasters may arise in the future, how should I prepare for these obstacles, and if I am experiencing a crisis now, how should I manage it?

As with the prior questions we examined, we will use a fictional composite example drawn from several companies I have led or advised. This example will show us how to apply the methodologies and tools from our blueprint to this disaster preparedness question. It is important to bear in mind that you likely will generate more than one card when you advance your process, and the concepts that we use in this chapter are just one example of how you can support your own activities.

Let us start our assessment phase for disaster preparedness by exploring the problems or opportunities that exist for our business that we could potentially address. This topic is likely to be far more oriented to problems than opportunities. Therefore, this assessment begins with the problems (and opportunities, if any) related to disaster preparedness for the business. For each problem or opportunity, we ask the detailed questions related to background and context, impact on future success or failure, constraints and expected benefits with solving the problem or meeting the opportunity, and options for solving the problem or meeting the opportunity. An example of one outcome from this assessment phase for exploring disaster preparedness and management options to create the conditions for success based on our fictional company is shown in Table 10.1.

PROBLEM AND OPPORTUNITY CARD— DISASTER PREPAREDNESS EXAMPLE

Problem/Opportunity Title	Disaster Preparedness Processes and Model
Problem/Opportunity Summary	Our business does not have a way to look at disasters and risks—or appropriate responses and mitigation plans—in an organized and comprehensive manner.
Background/Context	We believe that our business is underprepared to face disasters and risks that may arise in the years ahead (based on our experience with navigating COVID-19 remote work) and want to be better prepared.
Impact and Alignment to Future Success or Failure	If we have an organized model for examining and creating response plans for potential disasters and risks, including urgent threats, we can ensure that our business will be in a better position when issues arise.
Constraints on Solving/ Meeting	We cannot allow the solving of this problem and opportunity to distract us from our other higher-priority initiatives, but we need to advance this problem and opportunity in the medium term.

continued

Benefits of Solving/ Meeting	If we are more organized about disaster preparedness, we will be able to respond to disasters and risks that arise.
Options for Solving/ Meeting	We need to establish and operate a process and model for comprehensive disaster preparedness, including the following: identifying, assessing, and prioritizing potential disasters and risks; developing response and mitigation plans for the potential disasters and risks; creating an approach for managing urgent threats; and reviewing, experiencing, and updating the disaster assessments and response and mitigation plans.
Applicable Category	Disaster Preparedness
Prioritization	Medium—subject to decision-making process
Status	Awaiting decision-making about prioritization

Table 10.1. Problem and Opportunity Card—Disaster Preparedness Example

Next, we move from analysis and conceptualization to decision-making about planning for the resolution of disaster preparedness problems based on prioritization of our problems, opportunities, and solution pathways. Then we use the same two-step process to evaluate and prioritize, taking our problem and opportunity card example from Table 10.1 and determining potential planning and implementation priorities as shown in Table 10.2. The result in this scenario is that this card does not rank in the top five priorities for planning and implementation. This means we will defer both planning prioritization and implementation timing.

DECISION-MAKING STAGE-GATES—
DISASTER PREPAREDNESS EXAMPLE

Problem/ Opportunity Title	Disaster Preparedness Processes and Model	
Stage-Gate #	Questions to Answer	Result
Stage-Gate 1	• Question 1: Does the problem or opportunity cause a loss of revenue, loss of profit margin, loss of employees, misalignment of our mission, or other potential failure? • Answer 1: Yes. If we have an organized model for examining and creating responses to potential and exigent disasters and risks, we can ensure that our business will be in a better position when issues arise. • Question 2: Does the solution represent an opportunity to increase revenue, margins, team stability, business alignment to mission, or future success? • Answer 2: Yes. If we have an organized model for examining and creating responses to potential and exigent disasters and risks, we can ensure the future stability of our business. • Question 3: Does the problem or opportunity merit potential prioritization despite not eliciting a "yes" to one of the preceding questions? • Answer 3: Not applicable, as the answers to both Question 1 and Question 2 are "yes."	Since the answer is "yes" to the first two questions, the problem and opportunity card will be moved to decision-making stage-gate 2.

continued

| Stage-Gate 2 | • Question 1: Can the problem be solved or an opportunity seized for a reasonable investment of resources and within a reasonable timeline?

• Answer 1: Yes, we believe that with very limited time, we can establish a process and model to guide these activities.

• Question 2: Should we prioritize the solving of the problem or the seizing of the opportunity as one of our top five priorities to position the business for success and/or avoid failure?

• Answer 2: No, this problem/opportunity is not as critical as our existing top five priorities (as these top five will help us become a stronger business and ready for disasters and risks, but it is certainly in our top ten priorities). | Since the answer is "no" to one of our questions, the problem and opportunity card will be moved to lower-priority planning and advanced only as our higher-priority initiatives proceed through planning and implementation. |

Table 10.2. Decision-Making Stage-Gates—Disaster Preparedness Example

Our example provides a result that is a second-tier problem or opportunity. It is not one of our five highest priorities, but it is within our top ten problems and opportunities. We could, as time permits, proceed to planning with our methodology by creating an initiative planning charter with each of the key elements. We will need to consider how to ensure this proposed change occurs to create a better foundation for our business, our team, and our stakeholders. Similarly, we need to ensure that implementation timeline estimates are reasonable in the context of other activities and our business culture, given that this problem is not one of our highest priorities. An example of this planning process in action through an initiative planning charter follows in Table 10.3.

INITIATIVE PLANNING CHARTER—
DISASTER PREPAREDNESS EXAMPLE

Initiative Title	Disaster Preparedness Processes and Model
Problem/ Opportunity and Initiative Summary	Establish and operate a process and model for comprehensive disaster preparedness, including identifying, assessing, and prioritizing potential disasters and risks; developing response and mitigation plans for the potential disasters and risks; creating an approach for managing urgent threats; and reviewing, experiencing, and updating the disaster assessments and response and mitigation plans
Planning Leader	Imani Adebayo
Planning Team Members	Imani Adebayo Javier Soto Grace Chang Camila Martinez Johan Johansson Sean Williams Gabrielle Turner
Key Implementation Steps	• Develop and draft a high-level process and model for disaster assessment and preparedness • Finalize initial process and model for disaster assessment and preparedness • Conduct disaster and risk identification, assessment, and prioritization exercise • Conduct disaster response and mitigation planning exercise • Begin formal disaster preparedness plan documentation • Finalize formal disaster preparedness plan with management team • Review and approve disaster preparedness plan with governance team
Resources Needed	Time for the management team to develop process, model, and details and to apply this process, model, and details

Communications Strategy and Steps	Develop talking points for governance team about initiative and their roles with planning and implementation
Key Implementation Timelines	• + ~10 days—Develop a draft high-level process and model for disaster assessment and preparedness • + ~10 days—Finalize initial process and model for disaster assessment and preparedness • + ~10 days—Conduct disaster and risk identification, assessment, and prioritization exercise • + ~7 days—Conduct disaster response and mitigation planning exercise • + ~7 days—Begin formal disaster preparedness plan documentation • + ~15 days—Finalize formal disaster preparedness plan with management team • + ~15 days—Review and approve disaster preparedness plan with governance team

Table 10.3. Initiative Planning Charter—Disaster Preparedness Example

With planning complete (albeit at some point in the future since this was not one of our five highest priorities), we move to the most critical step in the process: implementation. We rely on our initiative planning charter tool to help us jump-start the process. Whenever we decide that we should move to implementation, we designate the leader, empower a team, delineate resources, establish an implementation monitoring protocol, develop a schedule, establish a mechanism for identifying and managing unforeseen issues and obstacles, and determine the required final activity for initial completion. As with the planning charter, we need to consider how to ensure this initiative will be positive for the business, our team members, and stakeholders. Similarly, we need to ensure the implementation charter is updated as issues and obstacles occur, including adjusting dates for execution while keeping reasonable timelines.

An example of this planning process in action through an initiative implementation charter—with some very distant timelines based on its later start given its lower priority level—follows in Table 10.4.

INITIATIVE IMPLEMENTATION CHARTER— DISASTER PREPAREDNESS EXAMPLE

Initiative Title	Disaster Preparedness Processes and Model
Problem/ Opportunity and Initiative Summary	Establish and operate a process and model for comprehensive disaster preparedness, including identifying, assessing, and prioritizing potential disasters and risks; developing response and mitigation plans for the potential disasters and risks; creating an approach for managing urgent threats; and reviewing, experiencing, and updating the disaster assessments and response and mitigation plans
Implementation Leader	Imani Adebayo
Implementation Team Members	Imani Adebayo Javier Soto Grace Chang Camila Martinez Johan Johansson Sean Williams Gabrielle Turner
Implementation Resources	Time for the management team to develop process, model, and details and to apply this process, model, and details
Implementation Monitoring Protocol	Status updates during management team and governance team meetings

continued

Key Implementation Steps and Schedule	• August 1 (next year)—Launch of initiative • August 10—Develop and draft high-level process and model for disaster assessment and preparedness • August 20—Finalize initial process and model for disaster assessment and preparedness • September 1—Conduct disaster and risk identification, assessment, and prioritization exercise • September 8—Conduct disaster response and mitigation planning exercise • September 15—Begin formal disaster preparedness plan documentation • September 30—Finalize formal disaster preparedness plan with management team • October 15—Review and approve disaster preparedness plan with governance team
Issues/Obstacles Encountered and Resulting Implementation Plan Changes	None encountered to date (and no changes to plan)
Final Activity Required for Initial Implementation Completion	Review and approve disaster preparedness plan by governance team

Table 10.4. Initiative Implementation Charter—Disaster Preparedness Example

In this chapter, we explored disaster planning as one of the eight critical and strategic decision categories for small- and medium-sized businesses. I hope this chapter encourages you to explore the potential disasters and risks that could challenge your business. By applying this streamlined methodology and our tools, you can change the way you examine, analyze, and develop responses to potential disasters and risks to position your business for future successes.

IN REVIEW

What did we learn from this chapter?

1. Utilizing lessons learned from government-directed business continuity management in a streamlined approach suitable for small- and medium-sized businesses, there are three important themes to help you determine how prepared you should be:

   a. Identify, assess, and prioritize potential disasters and risks

   b. Develop response and mitigation plans for the potential disasters and risks

   c. Review, experience, and update the disaster assessments and plans

2. The process of identifying, assessing, and prioritizing the potential disasters and risks that exist for your business includes:

   a. Conducting a thorough process to identify potential disasters and risks that could impact critical business functions or business outcomes

   b. Connecting the disasters and risks that are either derived or interdependent

   c. Examining and estimating the likelihood and impact of each disaster or risk

   d. Prioritizing the disasters and risks based on the combined impact and likelihood

   e. Producing a comprehensive and prioritized list of disasters and risks, their interrelationships, likelihood of occurrence, and associated potential impacts

3. Plans for continuity or resumption of operations for each of the disasters and risks could require significant planning and

investment, including training key personnel to fill critical roles when other key personnel are absent, implementing technology backup and restoration measures, establishing remote work options, establishing secondary operations centers, identifying alternative suppliers, and other tasks (as well as the communications that support these response activities).

4. You should regularly review and update your plans based on thoughtful reflection related to the changes in risks and your mitigation plans. You should do this based on your operational experiences because the struggles you face in your daily life often offer the best opportunities to identify potential disasters and how to mitigate the associated impacts.

To help you get ready for the work on disaster preparedness you will be doing soon, take a moment to answer the following four questions to help you determine how to best prepare for the potential disasters and risks that you and your business might face.

FOR FURTHER EXPLORATION

How do you plan to manage disasters that your business might face?

_____

_____

_____

_____

What disasters have you faced and what did you change as a result?

_____

_____

_____

_____

What disasters are you prepared to face? What disasters are you not ready to face?

_____

_____

_____

_____

What steps should you take to be better prepared for new disasters?

_____

_____

_____

_____

11

BUILT TO OUTLAST

"One of the things we often miss in succession planning
is that it should be gradual and thoughtful, with lots of
sharing of information and knowledge and perspective,
so that it's almost a nonevent when it happens."

—ANNE M. MULCAHY

Few thoughts are more difficult for owners and executives of small- and medium-sized businesses to contemplate than how their business or businesses will function without their knowledge, energy, and capabilities. Maybe that is why a staggering number of business owners and executives tend to ignore succession planning entirely or fail to take it beyond a narrow view of emergency situations. This lack of succession planning often stretches beyond replacing ourselves. It can also extend to our entire management teams.

Have you established a plan for who will take on your roles and functions to lead your business if you are unable to work for a short period of time without any warning? Have you developed a longer-term plan for the composition of the management team when you decide to retire but your business continues to function? Do you have plans for either short-term or long-term refilling of other key management team roles? What is the process you follow to make these emergency and long-term succession plans—and are the two plans integrated? If you have not established these plans or processes to support their construction, why have you not worked to ensure that your business is not just built to last, but built to outlast you?

When you are involved in building and sustaining a business, your goal for your business without you operating it may be different from the goals of your peers for their business. Perhaps you want the business to continue operating and provide an income source for your business partners, team members, or your family. Maybe you want the business to provide professional growth opportunities for your business partners, members of your team, or family members. Or it may be that you want the business you created to become part of a larger organization to provide more stability and a lasting impact. Whatever your preference, good succession planning will help you achieve your goal.

Ignoring Reality

Unfortunately, the builders of businesses tend to ignore the practical realities of developing realistic and reasonable plans to support succession during emergencies or over the longer-term. You have likely heard the statistics like those produced by Bank of America's Private Wealth Management Group, U.S. Trust. Their 2015 survey of high-net-worth individuals indicated that 61 percent of high-net-worth business owners did not have a succession plan.[18] Or maybe you have seen the often-cited data from the 2019 Successful Transgenerational Entrepreneurship Practices (or STEP) Global Family Business Survey (conducted in affiliation with KPMG).

---

18   "2015 U.S. Trust Insights on Wealth and Worth Survey," U.S. Trust, p. 67, https://www.privatebank.bankofamerica.com/publish/content/application/pdf/GWMOL/USTp_ARTNTGDB_2016-05.pdf.

That organization found that 70 percent of the family business leaders surveyed indicated that they did not have a formal succession plan in place.[19]

The group of expert business leaders that we surveyed—as leaders in their fields—tended to be better prepared than the groups of high-networth individuals and family business leaders that were studied by U.S. Trust and STEP, but only narrowly so. Figure 11.1 shows that 50 percent of these leaders had some type of succession plan. Among this group, the results were less than optimal; only 21 percent had both temporary (or emergency) and long-term succession plans, while 17 percent had only emergency succession plans, 10 percent had only long-term succession plans, and 2 percent had some other type of succession plan.

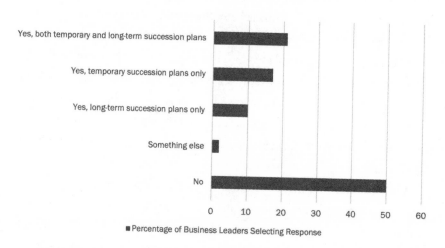

Figure 11.1

While we may not like the thought of disappearing from this life or the thought of one or more of our key management team members falling prey to the same fate, you or a key member of your team may

19   Andrea Calabro and Alfredo Valentino, "STEP 2019 Global Family Business Survey," Successful Transgenerational Entrepreneurship Practices (STEP) Project, 2019, 12, https://assets.kpmg/content/dam/kpmg/sa/pdf/2020/step-2019-global-family-business-survey-report.pdf.

pass away before your work is done. There is a stronger possibility that one or more of your leading team members may decide to pursue a new opportunity without much warning. There is an even stronger possibility—if your business was built to last—that you and your best talent will retire from the business. In the emergency scenarios that are thrust upon us by accident, ill health, or career choices, having a short-term succession plan can ensure continuity of business operations—just like your disaster response plans, but for your talent. For the longer-term retirement or resignations with significant advance notice, having a robust longer-range succession plan allows your business to live through these departures as nonevents.

The need for succession planning was made very clear to me in the early years of my first business venture. I was living and working in a university town in the heart of the Appalachian Mountains. The trade-off for gaining contemplative time for deep thinking without distraction was spending more time in cars and on planes to meet with current and prospective clients and partners. Unfortunate consequences of this need to travel tended to occur in the fall and winter when I found myself—more often than one might hope—trying to steer around deer that decided to make an ill-timed interstate highway crossing or attempting to regain control of my vehicle when black ice ended up covering bridges on those same highways.

One autumn morning near the end of peak foliage season, I was driving to a meeting several hours from the office. About an hour into the drive, I saw in my peripheral vision a large deer jumping over a guardrail from an uphill angle—right into the front passenger corner of the car I was driving. The car began spinning. It made full 360-degree revolutions for what seemed like an eternity. (By my count, it made at least four-and-a-half spins before landing in the median facing the opposite way from the direction I had been traveling.) If you have been in a car crash, you know the feeling I experienced of time being suspended. I received a very powerful message from that crash: You may not be here tomorrow, so you need to plan for that scenario. I did five things after that event: apologized to my wife (then my girlfriend), got the car repaired, increased my personal life and disability insurance coverages, obtained key person insurance at the business, and developed a succession plan, which was initially focused only on emergency situations.

As my business journey continued, new ventures were created, some businesses were acquired by publicly traded market leaders, and others were merged into consolidated opportunities. As a result, I had the opportunity to work in and advise various scales of organizations from two-person partnerships to exchange-listed giants. The best-performing of these companies—the ones that had the happiest teams and the best profitability—were the ones that understood that emergency and long-term succession planning were two equally important components of their operations and were most effective when implemented from integrated playbooks. Both types of planning merit a little more explanation before we examine how to build truly integrated succession plans.

Emergency Succession Plans

Emergency succession plans are usually fairly simple—especially when compared to long-term succession plans, which we will detail momentarily. These emergency plans are meant to be temporary in their application as a bridge to a more permanent solution (which could actually also be part of your long-term succession plans). These plans, as you would guess, are invoked when something abrupt happens—a death, a disability, an immediate resignation, and the like—and there are roles and functions that need to be filled and ably performed urgently.

For many organizations, their emergency plans consist of which current team member will be called upon to fill the role of a second team member—for a short period of time—if that second team member becomes unavailable. Other organizations take a slightly more nuanced approach in which the functions of a team member who is unavailable may be shared by multiple team members who may be more knowledgeable on certain areas of the functions under the purview of the team member who is out of the picture than any one single individual.

Long-Term Succession Plans

Long-term succession plans are far more complex. When you really want to make sure that your business outlasts you, your business partners, and your best managers, the process of creating and advancing long-term succession plans requires far more work than emergency succession plans. After all, these plans are meant to serve your business over the long haul, and it may take years to determine what changes might be needed (unless events overtake the long-term transition strategies).

The businesses that develop and carry out long-term succession plans with the greatest success know there is a critical difference between conducting assessments to simply assigning names to titles, conducting assessments, and preparing for transitions by gradually supporting implementations to make the handoff to the next set of leaders. If you do long-term succession planning in an organized and rational way, your emergency succession plans will become part of your long-term succession plans and vice versa.

Integrated Plans

The real value of an integrated succession plan is that it allows you to guide both the short-term responses to events that arise and the long-term gradual transitions you hope to be able to achieve—absent the drama and trauma. As a result, these plans allow you to avoid having your future plans derailed by near-term issues that occur. These emergency successions can be interim steps to a brighter future with a longer-term plan already linked to the emergency plan.

Based on my work with a host of small- and medium-sized businesses on succession planning, I have some valuable insights you can use to help you and your business. Three elements are critical to forging successful integrated and comprehensive succession plans:

1. Identify business needs, assess options and gaps, and determine viable pathways

2. Prepare your succession plans and determine associated required actions

3. Move forward with your plans and actions, review plans, and update as needed

Needs, Options, Gaps, and Pathways

When you start the process of integrated succession planning, it is important to remember that succession is not about you—or even just replacing you. It is about what (and who) is needed to fill the key roles and functions in the business that you and likely other members of your team perform, both temporarily and longer-term. As much as possible, try to leave emotions and sentimental thoughts out of the planning and thinking process.

Trusting yourself and your team is a key part of our approach. And because succession planning is about your team, I recommend that this process be conducted by the management team and that the governance team reviews the management team's analysis. Granted, if you are the sole owner or only manager, you may be doing some of the analysis and decision-making by yourself. If you do not have a management team or a formal governance team (or even if you do), you likely will want to engage your top outside advisors, too.

As you (and most likely your team) begin this planning, it is important to recall how you built a team around your strengths or those of your business partners or management team. You brought in people whose strengths were complementary to those of the existing team. As you do succession planning, you need to consider the strengths and weaknesses of your core team of successors and build around those capabilities.

This assessment process may require a mental reset—not just to consider your own mortality and its consequences if you have not done succession planning previously, but also to reassess the roles and functions that should be vested in one individual within a business. Consider what roles and responsibilities—either in emergency circumstances or in the future—should be split among multiple team members. The fact is, it might take a team to replace you or some of your most talented team members.

That is where the assessment work begins—with a determination of what your business needs in terms of roles and functions, both today and tomorrow, and the associated knowledge and skills to fill those roles and functions. For instance, if you or another one of your Professional Swiss Army Knife team members who perform multiple roles are unavailable—be it short-term or long-term—you may need more than just one individual to backfill for that person. This is where succession planning for roles and functions can diverge. As an example, if you are in the CEO role, you may be the lead on sales, financial management, and product management, which are three separate functions combined in one role. But if you were not in this role, it is unlikely that these three functions would all be vested in the CEO position. Therefore, when you document business needs, it is important to document the roles *and* the functions because, in many instances, the future functional assignments will not align with the current roles.

After you document the roles and functions, it is time to assess the composition of your existing team compared to the documented needs for roles and functions. This will help determine the emergency and long-term succession options. In performing this assessment, you will also need to assess the interests of the team members in either the temporary or long-range opportunities. For this reason, it is important to be precise in your communications with your team about your intent, the interest each team member has in fulfilling roles and functions, and the fact that the succession plans may evolve over time, which may mean that plans and trajectories for their alignment to future roles and functions may change, too. A lack of clarity in communications can undermine the validity of the plans, set up expectations for future sustained job opportunities that may be unrealistic, and potentially lead to the loss of team members who are important to your business today and your plans for tomorrow. Thus, it is important to be very careful and very clear during both assessment and planning.

It is important to look at your entire team, which might even include members of your governance team who are not full-time employees, when considering potential alignment to roles and functions. Some of the best successors—for both temporary and permanent assignments—could be members of your personal security council. After all, you trust them to advise you, and you might find that some of these individuals are the best successor candidates. Finally, as we noted during the management team discussion, it is important to look at your options for filling roles and functions with individuals who may not be carbon copies of the current role and function performers.

When you are conducting this analysis, you will no doubt find there are gaps between the existing roles and functions and the current capabilities of your team. For this reason, it is important to consider the potential future capabilities of your team, including what gaps can be filled through growth with training and knowledge transfer. This road map for developing future capabilities can support not just succession planning, but also improve your operational outcomes today. Sometimes, not all of the gaps can be filled by training. In those circumstances, it is important to decide how to achieve the temporary succession needs with your team and outside advisors while you consider how to potentially recruit new talent to the organization to improve the odds of success for your long-term succession plan. Depending on the financial position of your business, it may or may not be practical to pursue these recruitment activities today. And, if it is not practical, it is quite reasonable to simply turn your eye toward potential future hires.

Document Plans and Actions

After you and your team have completed your assessment, it is important to thoroughly document both the emergency and long-term succession plans, as well as the actions that are needed. Such actions might include training, knowledge transfer, mentorship, ownership opportunities, other compensation incentives, or recruitment of new team members for significant functional succession gaps to ensure these plans can be implemented successfully when needed. After you and your management team members finalize the documentation, you will want to review these plans with your governance team to obtain their guidance and feedback (and, most importantly, to have them double-check the plans).

In addition to the formal documentation, there should be clear communication with the members of your team about their parts (or lack thereof) in both the near-term and long-term succession plans. For the team members who are important to the integrated succession plan, you may want to consider new or additional ownership opportunities and sustained duration incentive plans to ensure these most valuable team members are willing to stay for the foreseeable future. For the team members who may not be currently projected to play significant parts in the succession plans, you need to be prepared for departures, because their exclusion from or small parts in the plans may not align with their vision for their future at your business. It may be important to consider how to provide additional opportunities or incentives to keep them happy and engaged if they are important members of your team.

Implement Plans and Actions (and Updates)

With your integrated succession plan—consisting of emergency and long-term elements—finalized, you can begin the process of the training, knowledge transfer, and mentorship necessary to effectuate it. With your foresight, you should be able to make any transition of responsibilities for the long-term succession incremental. This process, in all likelihood, should be able to support better performance if temporary succession plans are triggered in the interim.

As you advance these actions to support the plans, you also should continually assess how the training, knowledge transfer, and mentorship activities are proceeding. If things are not going well and it looks like your plans may have been a little optimistic on potential future capability development among the team for certain roles or functions, you may need to update your plans. Most companies reexamine their succession plans no less than annually, and as circumstances warrant, to ensure the needs and potential fits are still valid and aligned.

Applying the Blueprint

Some of you may be wondering how to apply our methodologies and tools to this eighth critical and strategic decision question: What happens to my business and my family's livelihood when it is time for me (or key management team members) to retire—or, worse, meet an untimely demise?

As with the prior questions we examined, we will use a fictional composite example developed from several companies I have led or advised. This example will show us how to apply the methodologies and tools from our blueprint to this succession planning question. It is important to bear in mind that you will likely generate more than one card when you advance your process, and the concepts we use in this chapter are just one example of how you can support your own activities.

Let us start our assessment phase for succession planning by exploring the problems or opportunities that exist for our business that it could potentially address. In this area, it is likely to be far more oriented to problems than opportunities. As a result, this assessment begins with the problems (and opportunities, if any) related to succession planning for the business. For each problem or opportunity, we ask the detailed questions related to background and context, impact on future success or failure, constraints and expected benefits with solving the problem or meeting the opportunity, and options for solving the problem or meeting the opportunity. An example of one outcome from this assessment phase for exploring succession planning options to create the conditions for success based on our fictional company is shown in Table 11.1.

PROBLEM AND OPPORTUNITY CARD—
SUCCESSION PLANNING EXAMPLE

Problem/ Opportunity Title	Integrated Succession Plan to Support Emergency and Long-Term Succession
Problem/ Opportunity Summary	Our business does not have a long-term succession plan, nor strategies to produce one. In addition, our emergency succession plan is limited to who serves in the roles of CEO and CFO if one of those leaders is unavailable. So, we believe we need to develop an integrated succession plan.
Background/Context	We have not prepared the business well for transition of leadership from our current management team (most of whom are in their mid-to-late fifties) or for emergency succession needs for the majority of our management team.
Impact and Alignment to Future Success or Failure	If we have an integrated process and model for succession planning, our business will be ready to face both emergency situations and the longer-term leadership sustainability issues.
Constraints on Solving/Meeting	We cannot allow the solving of this problem and opportunity to distract us from our other higher priority initiatives, but we need to advance this problem and opportunity in the mid-term (as every day that we do not could be the day that emergency succession plans are needed).
Benefits of Solving/ Meeting	If we focus on succession planning—both short-term and long-term—we actually develop a stronger team to operate the business in the years ahead.

Options for Solving/ Meeting	We need to establish and operate an integrated succession planning process and model that allows us to identify business succession needs, assess options and gaps among our current team, determine viable pathways for short-term and long-term succession, develop short-term and long-term succession plans, determine associated required actions to support the plans, finalize the plans, move forward with the required actions, and review/update the plans.
Applicable Category	Succession Planning
Prioritization	Medium—subject to decision-making process
Status	Awaiting decision-making about prioritization

Table 11.1. Problem and Opportunity Card—Succession Planning Example

Next, we move from analysis and conceptualization to decision-making about planning for the resolution of succession planning problems based on prioritization of our problems, opportunities, and solution pathways. Then we use the same two-step process to evaluate and prioritize, taking our problem and opportunity card example from Table 11.1 and determining potential planning and implementation priorities as shown in Table 11.2. The result in this scenario is that this card does not rank in the top five priorities for planning and implementation, which means we likely will defer both planning prioritization and implementation timing.

DECISION-MAKING STAGE-GATES— SUCCESSION PLANNING EXAMPLE

Problem/ Opportunity Title	Integrated Succession Plan to Support Emergency and Long-Term Succession	
Stage-Gate #	**Questions to Answer**	**Result**
Stage-Gate 1	• Question 1: Does the problem or opportunity cause a loss of revenue, loss of profit margin, loss of employees, misalignment of our mission, or other potential failure? • Answer 1: Yes. Currently, our business is ill-equipped to handle emergency situations and the longer-term leadership sustainability issues, which could lead to a business failure in a time of crisis. • Question 2: Does the solution represent an opportunity to increase revenue, margins, team stability, business alignment to mission, or future success? • Answer 2: Yes. If we have an integrated process and model for succession planning, our business will be ready to face both emergency situations and the longer-term leadership sustainability issues. • Question 3: Does the problem or opportunity merit potential prioritization despite not eliciting a "yes" to one of the preceding questions? • Answer 3: Not applicable, as the answers to both Question 1 and Question 2 are "yes."	Since the answer is "yes" to the first two questions, the problem and opportunity card will be moved to decision-making stage-gate 2.

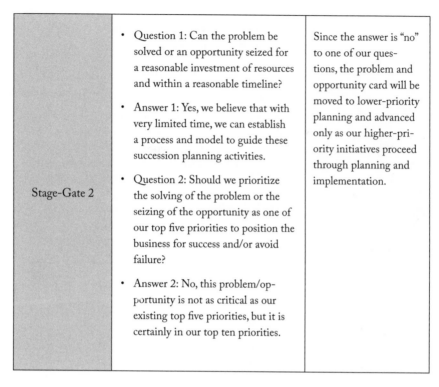

| Stage-Gate 2 | • Question 1: Can the problem be solved or an opportunity seized for a reasonable investment of resources and within a reasonable timeline?

• Answer 1: Yes, we believe that with very limited time, we can establish a process and model to guide these succession planning activities.

• Question 2: Should we prioritize the solving of the problem or the seizing of the opportunity as one of our top five priorities to position the business for success and/or avoid failure?

• Answer 2: No, this problem/opportunity is not as critical as our existing top five priorities, but it is certainly in our top ten priorities. | Since the answer is "no" to one of our questions, the problem and opportunity card will be moved to lower-priority planning and advanced only as our higher-priority initiatives proceed through planning and implementation. |

Table 11.2. Decision-Making Stage-Gates—Succession Planning Example

Our example provides a result that is a second-tier problem or opportunity. It is not one of our five highest priorities, but it is one of our top ten problems and opportunities. We could, if time permits, proceed to planning with our methodology by creating an initiative planning charter with each of the key elements. We will need to consider how to ensure this proposed change to create a better foundation for our business, our team, and our stakeholders occurs. Similarly, we need to ensure that implementation timeline estimates are reasonable in the context of other activities and our business culture, given this problem is not one of our highest priorities. An example of this planning process in action through an initiative planning charter follows in Table 11.3.

INITIATIVE PLANNING CHARTER— SUCCESSION PLANNING EXAMPLE

Initiative Title	Integrated Succession Plan
Problem/ Opportunity and Initiative Summary	Establish and operate an integrated succession planning process and model that allows us to: identify business succession needs; assess options and gaps among our current team; determine viable pathways for short-term and long-term succession; develop short-term and long-term succession plans; determine associated required actions to support the plans; finalize the plans; move forward with the required actions; and review/update the plans
Planning Leader	Gabrielle Turner
Planning Team Members	Gabrielle Turner Javier Soto Grace Chang Camila Martinez Sean Williams Ali Kamgar
Key Implementation Steps	• Develop process and model for integrated succession planning • Identify business succession needs (including both roles and functions) • Assess options and gaps among our current team • Determine viable pathways for short-term and long-term succession • Develop short-term and long-term succession plans • Determine associated required actions to support the plans • Finalize the plans with the management team • Review and approve integrated success plan with governance team • Launch plan and initiate required actions
Resources Needed	Time for the management team to develop process, model, and plan, as well as apply this process, model, and plan

Communications Strategy and Steps	Develop talking points for governance team about initiative and their roles with planning and implementation
Key Implementation Timelines	<ul><li>+ ~10 days—Develop process and model for integrated succession planning</li><li>+ ~15 days—Identify business succession needs (including both roles and functions)</li><li>+ ~15 days—Assess options and gaps among our current team</li><li>+ ~15 days—Determine viable pathways for short-term and long-term succession</li><li>+ ~15 days—Develop short-term and long-term succession plans</li><li>+ ~5 days—Determine associated required actions to support the plans</li><li>+ ~5 days—Finalize the plans with the management team</li><li>+ ~15 days—Review and approve integrated succession plan with governance team</li><li>+ ~5 days—Launch plan and initiate required actions</li></ul>

Table 11.3. Initiative Planning Charter—Succession Planning Example

With planning complete (albeit at some point in the future since this was not one of our five highest priorities), we move to the most critical step in the process: implementation. We rely on our initiative planning charter tool to help us jump-start the process. Whenever we decide we should move to implementation, we designate the leader, empower a team, delineate resources, establish an implementation monitoring protocol, develop a schedule, establish a mechanism for identifying and managing unforeseen issues and obstacles, and determine the required final activity for initial completion. As with the planning charter, we need to consider how to ensure this initiative will be positive for the business, our team members, and stakeholders. Similarly, we need to ensure the implementation charter is updated as issues and obstacles occur, including adjusting dates for execution while keeping reasonable timelines.

An example of this planning process in action through an initiative implementation charter—with some very distant timelines based on its later start given its lower priority level—follows in Table 11.4.

INITIATIVE IMPLEMENTATION CHARTER— SUCCESSION PLANNING EXAMPLE

Initiative Title	Integrated Succession Plan
Problem/ Opportunity and Initiative Summary	Establish and operate an integrated succession planning process and model that allows us to identify business succession needs, assess options and gaps among our current team, determine viable pathways for short-term and long-term succession, develop short-term and long-term succession plans, determine associated required actions to support the plans, finalize the plans, move forward with the required actions, and review/ update the plans
Implementation Leader	Gabrielle Turner
Implementation Team Members	Gabrielle Turner Javier Soto Grace Cheng Camila Martinez Sean Williams Ali Kamgar
Implementation Resources	Time for the management team to develop process, model, and plan, as well as apply this process, model, and plan
Implementation Monitoring Protocol	Status updates during management team and governance team meetings

Key Implementation Steps and Schedule	• November 1 (next year)—Launch initiative • November 11—Develop process and model for integrated succession planning • December 1—Identify business succession needs (including both roles and functions) • December 16—Assess options and gaps among our current team • January 16—Determine viable pathways for short-term and long-term succession • January 31—Develop short-term and long-term succession plans • February 6—Determine associated required actions to support the plans • February 12—Finalize the plans with the management team • February 28—Review and approve integrated succession plan with governance team • March 5—Launch plan and initiate required actions
Issues/Obstacles Encountered and Resulting Implementation Plan Changes	None encountered to date (and no changes to plan)
Final Activity Required for Initial Implementation Completion	Review and approve integrated succession plan by governance team

Table 11.4. Initiative Implementation Charter—Succession Planning Example

In this chapter, we examined succession planning as one of the eight critical and strategic decision categories for small- and medium-sized businesses. In doing so, I hope this chapter prompts you to consider developing (or if you are ahead of most of your fellow business leaders, updating) succession plans. Your succession plan should include both emergency and long-term plans as part of an integrated succession plan. This will help your business outlast you (if you want it to do so). By applying this streamlined methodology and our tools, you can change the way you examine, analyze, and develop succession plans to position your business for future successes.

IN REVIEW

What did we learn from this chapter?

1. Emergency and long-term succession planning are two equally important components and are best operated together as integrated succession plans. If you do long-term succession planning in an organized and rational way, your emergency succession plans become part of your long-term succession, and vice versa.

2. Emergency succession plans are meant to be temporary in their application as a bridge to a more permanent solution (which could also be part of your long-term succession plans). These emergency plans are invoked when something abrupt happens—a death, a disability, an immediate resignation, and the like—and roles and responsibilities need to be filled and ably performed urgently.

3. Long-term succession plans are far more complex, as there is a critical difference between simply assigning names to titles and conducting assessments, preparing for transitions, and gradually supporting implementations to make the handoff to the next set of leaders.

4. Three elements are critical for you and your business to forge successful integrated and comprehensive succession plans:

    a. Identify business needs, assess options and gaps, and determine viable pathways

b. Prepare your succession plans and determine associated required actions

c. Move forward with your plans and actions, review plans, and update as needed

5. It is important to be clear in your communications with your team about your intent, the interest each team member has in fulfilling roles and functions, their part in the plans, and the fact that the succession plans may evolve over time. A lack of clarity in communications can undermine the plans, set up expectations for future job opportunities that may be unrealistic, and worse, lead to the loss of team members.

To help you get ready for the succession planning work you will do soon, please take a moment to answer the following four questions to help determine how to best prepare for succession planning—both emergency and long-term—for you and your business.

FOR FURTHER EXPLORATION

What are your emergency and long-term succession plans? Are these plans integrated? If not, how could these plans be integrated?

_____

_____

_____

_____

What is missing from your succession plans today?

_____

_____

_____

_____

Who is involved in your succession planning process? Who else should be involved in your succession planning process?

_____

_____

_____

_____

What should you do to update your succession planning process and plans?

_____

_____

_____

_____

CONCLUSION

"The only way around is through."

—ROBERT FROST

As you know, the work of leading or helping to lead small- to medium-sized businesses is intense. It likely brings us great joy and, at times, some pain. For most of us, it fulfills our desire to be deeply engaged—intellectually, emotionally, and physically—during our waking hours. But it may shortchange us on sleeping hours and vacation hours. Many of us are so connected to our business or businesses that we find the lines between these organizations and our existence to be a bit blurred. We may feel as though we can never really check out, unplug, and decompress.

The fact that you opted to read this book (and have made it to the Conclusion) makes it clear that you want success for your business. We often obsess over external factors that can impact our businesses, but the reality is that it is the internal factors that make the difference between success and failure. The structural components you select and use to operate your business will ultimately do more to drive positive outcomes and help you to manage risks and threats than most of the other decisions or actions you take in your business.

You have the power to ensure that you and your businesses achieve success rather than fall prey to failure. You can achieve this if you focus on building your business better—from the inside. While reading this book, you benefited from the lessons learned from two decades of experience and deep research. This includes engagement with a diverse group of highly successful executive leaders who are recognized as experts in their industries and who verified the concepts set forth in the chapters in this book. Now, the tools are in your hands, and there is work to be done. If you continue to focus on the critical and strategic decisions you need to make to create the internal structures that propel success, you will build and rebuild your business to be stronger and reap the benefits of those efforts.

Whether your goal for your business or businesses is sustainment, growth, an exit, or something else, you and your team now have a simple framework—consisting of approaches, methodologies, and tools—for assessing, determining, planning, and implementing decisions about the internal structural components of your business for the years ahead. These resources will allow you to continue to successfully build jobs, teams, products, services, communities, wealth, or whatever else you do by helping you to improve your business from the inside.

Ideally, you are ready to apply what you have learned from each chapter and from your own reflections during the course of your reading. I hope you also feel better prepared to build and rebuild the internal structural components of your business as you pursue your goals for you, your team, and your business or businesses. Whenever you feel like your organization needs to improve its performance and internal structures, I encourage you to revisit the relevant chapters. The information in those chapters will help you and your team focus on the prioritized internal factors that will position your business for success in the years ahead.

While you and your team will ultimately determine which internal structures are important to your business, the eight most important inside categories that have been shown to impact success and failure from our research are:

- Governance models and governance team composition

- Management team models, composition, engagement, and compensation

- Adjustments and pivots

- Growth and infrastructure development

- Business disputes and breakups

- Acquisitions, mergers, exits, and other business transactions

- Disaster preparedness and management

- Succession planning

When you manage these internal structures, you will generally find that your business just seems to operate better (and you may sleep better and feel better, too). You will need to revisit these internal structures regularly (some more than others), since, as we all know, change happens.

As you go about the work of building and rebuilding your business with the support of your new methodologies and tools, remember to go beyond your personal context of experiences. Open your mind to a broader context and new approaches that leverage insights from others—both on your team and beyond. Consider the value of building from the ground up. Look at the importance of worrying productively and embracing change. Make the commitment to do the hard work—and trust the insights and instincts that you and your team bring to the activities of re-architecting and rebuilding your core business structures. After all, you are the users of the business at the center of this design-thinking exercise. Most importantly, focus on identifying problems, opportunities, and solution pathways, as this approach will keep you grounded in the initiatives you actually need to undertake.

One last point: Never get too comfortable. There will be instances when you may need to rebuild the internal structures that support your business multiple times. If you become complacent with your current success, you could miss out on the possibility of sustained success.

When you work through the methodologies for assessment, decision-making, planning, and implementation—by using the tools in this book or similar resources—consider focusing on the eight critical and strategic areas that make the difference between success and failure. Then judiciously add other internal factors you deem important. In doing so, remember to assess regularly. As situations warrant, make decisions on a regular schedule or when urgent matters require attention, and plan and implement only for the very small number of priorities you have decided are crucial to business performance. Consider leveraging the responses you provided at the end of each chapter as starting points for identifying problems, opportunities, and solution pathways. You may also want to consider whether the examples we provided might be helpful in some way to your business. Some of these concepts may be applicable, while others may not. Similarly, the examples that were priorities for our fictional business may or may not be priorities for your business, even if they are problems or opportunities for you and your businesses. Sometimes, however, these concepts may serve—along with your reflections—as a useful jump-start for your efforts.

As a final note, when this book was conceptualized, my vision was to leave you with a lasting resource to build strong internal structures to position your business for future successes. I hope it will be a resource that will assist you, your team, and your business in the years ahead.

Best of luck to you as you start building and rebuilding your business based on the structure of success!

ACKNOWLEDGMENTS

This book is the culmination of nearly fifty years of learning, more than twenty years of business experience, and more than seven years of concept development, research, and writing. Many people were vitally important to both the creation of this book and the pathway I traveled to develop and explore the ideas that are included within its pages.

First, I am deeply indebted and grateful to my family and friends, who help guide me, keep me grounded, and from whom I learn on a regular basis. Most notably, this includes my wife, Michelle Varga Esposito. Throughout our nearly twenty-five years together, she has shown me that my primary career path in life should be in business. This also includes my children, Natalie Esposito and Elizabeth Esposito, who have provided me with opportunities to teach and be taught every day since I became a parent. Many thanks go to my parents, Dr. Patrick Esposito and Caroline Esposito, for instilling a love of learning in me. As an engineer and psychologist respectively, they helped me to understand structural systems and that you need to consider the role of people in those systems. To my sister, Cara Esposito Gump, and her husband, J.D. Gump, thank you for our many conversations—most notably, our family business succession planning dialogues. To my in-laws, nieces, nephew, uncles, aunts, my late grandparents, cousins, and friends, those with us today and those who have passed on, many thanks for teaching me valuable lessons about life.

I also wish to thank my mentors and guides in life and in business. I am grateful to all of you for the time you invested in me. Beginning in my formative years, I had the benefit of great teachers who pushed me to do more—including, most notably, my junior high school math coach, Dr. Jane Michael. I was also aided by great mentors and advisors like Dr. William Collins, Ms. JoAnn Evans, Dr. Robert DiClerico, Dr. Carolyn Zinn, Dr. Enid Portnoy, and Dr. William Trumbull. During my undergraduate years, they all invested time and energy to help me find a way to serve others. Similarly, at University College, Oxford, Professor Hartmut Pogge von Strandmann and Dr. Leslie Mitchell helped foster my understanding of innovative research and engaging writing.

To my business partners, friends in business ventures, coworkers, investors, clients, employers, and colleagues, I have learned from each of you and am grateful for our time together. While there are far too many organizations and individuals with whom I have enjoyed working to list each by name, there are some that merit detailing based on their impact on my life and some of the concepts explored in this book.

As I was navigating my journey to business through public service, I was fortunate to work for Governor Bob Wise (both when he was a U.S. Congressman and later as governor of the state of West Virginia) and his team members—including Susan Small, Chip Slaven, Lowell Johnson, Tom Gavin, Nancy Minigh Gavin, Hubert Yang, Michael Garrison, Alexander Macia, and a host of others—as I first gained insights into organizational dynamics (and was also introduced to my wife by members of this team).

Some early clients, including the U.S. Department of Energy and multiple U.S. Department of Defense agencies, and early investors—my father (Pat), Bill Maloney, Richard Ross and Andy Zulauf (from the West Virginia Jobs Investment Trust), and Paul Batcheller (from PrairieGold Venture Partners)—provided the opportunity to start and grow Augusta Systems with a team that included my father, my wife, James Dobbs, Gina Dubbe, George Thomas, Jack Williams, Scott Zemerick, Michael Cole,

Clint Harvey, John Moody, Bruce Vest, and others. Perhaps most significantly, based on this phase of my business career, I owe more than I can ever repay to Gina Dubbe, who truly taught me how to operate and grow a small software start-up and transition it to its logical home.

Concurrently with the Augusta Systems journey, I had the opportunity to engage in building an advanced polymer composite products business called Resilient Technologies, and gained insights into manufacturing from working with Ali Manesh, Bob Lange, and Edward Hall, among many others, which has helped me to advise many other businesses with sophisticated production operations.

I was profoundly impacted by my work in the heavily regulated financial services sector as an executive officer and, later, an outside advisor to the team at MVB Financial Corp. and MVB Bank, including, most notably, working for Larry Mazza and alongside Donald Robinson, Kenneth Ash, Aly Goodwin Gregg, Amanda Curry, and many others.

My legal counsel experiences advising small- and medium-sized businesses have been a direct result of the amazing team at Spilman, Thomas & Battle, PLLC, including Michael Basile, David Ferretti, Michael Garrison, and (again), my wife, Michelle.

After several years away from the software industry (and missing what seemed like at least a quarter of a lifetime of evolution), I was fortunate to become involved with a number of new ventures that focused on creating innovative software and services offerings for clients and new market opportunities with great minds, including Matthew Milan, Jon Tirmandi, Nicholas Burling, and Mark Wise, among others. Working with these individuals—within the businesses they led—helped me to become even better prepared to support other new technology companies and also clients that seek to leverage new technologies for business needs.

I was also honored to have the opportunity to serve U.S. national security needs through work with U.S. Department of Defense leaders at the National Security Innovation Network (including directors Dr. Adam Jay Harrison, Morgan Plummer, and others) for the Civil-Military Innovation Institute (with Dr. Zenovy Wowczuk, Adam Hanasky, Mitch

Kusmier, and John Reisenweber, and others) and other contractors, the Army Applications Laboratory (including directors Col. (Ret.) Len Rosanoff, Col. Jay Wisham, and others) for Alion Science and Technology Corporation, now Huntington-Ingalls Industries (with Christopher Zember and Gregg Sypeck), and the U.S. Army Catalyst-Pathfinder Program (including Dr. Arwen DeCostanza, Dr. Anthony Pezzano, Lt. Col. (Ret.) Robert Dionisio, and others). In doing this meaningful work, I enjoyed working alongside some amazing teammates at ACME General Corp., including my childhood friend and ACME business partner, David Bonfili, as well as Ken Harbaugh, Eric Frey, Neal Wendt, Allen Grane, Gary Lawson, Beth Bossio, and Kirk Curry, among others.

To my YPO forum group, thank you. You all gave me the idea that some of my random musings might be book material.

Finally, many thanks to the team that helped me make this book a reality, including Greenleaf Book Group, *Inc.* magazine, and a host of friends who reviewed drafts along the way. I appreciate all your efforts. And to my editors—Diana Ceres, Lindsay Clark, Heather Stettler, Claudia Volkman, and Diana Coe—and the executive and project teams at Greenleaf, including Tanya Hall, Tyler LeBleu, Brian Welch, Chelsea Richards, Chase Quarterman, and Daniel Sandoval: I am impressed that you could take a writer of reports and developer of PowerPoint presentations and turn him into a serviceable writer in such a short time.

I am thankful for all of you!

INDEX

ABOUT THE AUTHOR

PATRICK ESPOSITO is an entrepreneur, business executive, attorney, advisor,
and board member (and most importantly, a
father and husband). He has helped to found,
lead, and advise small- and medium-sized
businesses in technology, consulting, retail,
banking, real estate, and other sectors, as
well as U.S. government organizations, for
more than two decades. During his career, Esposito has advised start-up
executive teams, family business owners, large publicly traded company
executive teams, and leaders in the U.S. Department of Defense.

Currently, Esposito serves as president of ACME General Corp., a
leading public sector innovation advisory business based in New York,
Austin, and Morgantown, West Virginia. He also serves as counsel with
Spilman Thomas & Battle, a Mid-Atlantic regional law firm. Esposito
recently launched Initiative Labs LLC to help small- and medium-sized
business leaders apply the approaches, methodologies, and tools from this
book to create the conditions for success in their business ventures.

Prior to his role as an advisor and attorney focused on supporting this
broad range of clients, Esposito held many different positions. He was a

co-founder and CEO of a family-led, venture-backed software company (Augusta Systems, Inc.) based in Morgantown, West Virginia. That firm pivoted three times, became an early Internet of Things pioneer, made the *Inc.* 500 list, and was acquired by a publicly traded, multinational technology company. Esposito was a co-founder and board member of an innovative vehicle components technology company (Resilient Technologies LLC) based in Wausau, Wisconsin. The firm was acquired by a leading vehicle products company. He was also the chief legal and risk officer in a publicly traded, high-growth financial services company.

Esposito graduated from the Georgetown University Law Center with a juris doctor degree. Prior to attending Georgetown, Esposito earned a master of studies degree in modern history at the University of Oxford, England, studying on a Rotary Ambassadorial Scholarship. Esposito graduated cum laude from West Virginia University (WVU) and the WVU Honors Program with two bachelor of arts degrees in four majors—the first in economics and political science, and the second in history and international studies—under a WVU Foundation Scholarship. Esposito and his wife, Michelle, and their two daughters, Natalie and Elizabeth, reside in Morgantown, West Virginia. This location enables an efficient existence in a university city and supports a life that focuses on family and business clients.